'In a competitive world of sameness, noise and low trust, Rob Brown's excellent guide to reputation building gives busy corporate executives and professionals the definitive guide to standing out in a crowd.'

Jeff Black, President & CEO, Black Sheep Inc

'Over 100 practical strategies to get your name out there. Just do 10% of what Rob Brown tells, and in a year's time your life, reputation and positioning will be completely transformed.'

Daniel Barnett, Barrister, Broadcaster and Keynote Speaker

'Simply brilliant. A *tour de force* of why and how to build your reputation. An invaluable and intensely practical must-read.'

Steve Pipe, Author of *The World's Most Inspiring Accountants*

'As a thought leader, your reputation is your most valuable asset. Without it, you have no trust and no credibility and no business. If you're an expert looking to stand out in a competitive industry, this is your blueprint to success.'

Warren Knight, Social Media Strategist, Social Sales Strategist and Award-Winning Entrepreneur

'If you want to succeed in business today, you need a strong reputation; people need to know, trust and like you. In this book, Rob Brown sets out exactly how you can stand out giving over 100 strategies that you can use to build your most valuable career and business asset. Rob knows what he is talking about so read this book and set your sights on being the number one go-to person in your field.'

Gavin Ingham, Author of *Motivate People*

'Standing up and standing out for something is one of the few paths to success in life. Few people achieve this, usually because they don't know exactly how. This book by Rob Brown gives you the answers to practically make that happen – a must-read for anyone who wants to get on in life.'

Geoff Burch, International Business Expert, TV presenter and Bestselling Author

'To excel in any business or industry you need to make sure you create and maintain an excellent personal reputation. In this book Rob shares in detail how you go about achieving that brilliantly and gives you a roadmap to success.'

Simon Chaplin, Founder, Socks Up Simon www.socksupsimon.com

'You can't buy a good reputation and building one needn't cost you a fortune either. Rob Brown walks his talk and his reputation will inspire you as you read this book. Make reading it your first step in your journey to a great reputation.'

Robert Ashton, The Barefoot Entrepreneur

'Reputation matters! If you aspire to rise to the top of your "career game", then Rob Brown's book is a must-read for you. This brilliant book guides you on how to strategically create and market your personal brand so you stand out in the competitive world of business as a leader and corporate influencer.'

Adèle McLay, Business Growth Strategist, Entrepreneur, Investor, Keynote Speaker, and Author

'If you want to stand out from the crowd and get ahead, then Rob Brown's excellent guide will give you all the tools you need to build a world-class reputation and network that will get you through any doors.'

Nigel Risner, Award-Winning Leadership Speaker

'Understanding, respecting and leveraging your reputation are key to having a successful career. It's what got you where you are and what will shape your future. This book by renowned reputation authority Rob Brown helps by giving you the tools to take charge of this most valuable asset.'

Adam Harris, Vistage Chair, Business Coach and Speaker

'I have thoroughly enjoyed watching Rob's TEDx Talk on YouTube (twice!), listening to him being interviewed on podcasts, and hearing him talk live. So I eagerly grabbed hold of a copy of his new book at the earliest opportunity. Within minutes of scanning through it I found a brilliant nugget, which I highlighted, and I soon found more. I loved those sudden rushes of dopamine. Rob's book is hugely practical and he writes with delightful playfulness. I'm very happy to recommend it highly.'

Christopher John Payne, Founder, Effort-Free Media

'In a world where building your personal brand matters more than ever before, Rob Brown has produced a book full of practical advice for those individuals who understand that managing their reputation cannot merely be left to chance.'

Grant Leboff, CEO, StickyMarketing.com

'If you want to be an influential and impactful leader, then you are going to need a strong reputation and a strong network. This insightful and practical book will give you the tools and methods you need to build both.'

Simon Hazeldine, Bestselling Author of *Neuro-Sell: How Neuroscience Can Power Your Sales Success*

'In his brilliant new book on building your personal reputation, Rob Brown says that reputation is "what people say about you behind your back". If luck is where preparation meets opportunity, then building your reputation intentionally makes you luckier as you are better prepared, and more opportunities will find you, not the other way round.'

David Gilroy, Director of Stuff & Things, Conscious Solutions

'Rob Brown's reputation book will become a bible for anyone serious about developing their career prospects.'

Robert Craven, Managing Director, The Directors Center

BUILD YOUR REPUTATION

GROW YOUR PERSONAL BRAND FOR CAREER AND BUSINESS SUCCESS

ROB BROWN

WILEY

This edition first published 2016
© 2016 Rob Brown

Registered office
John Wiley & Sons Ltd, The Atrium, Southern Gate, Chichester, West Sussex, PO19 8SQ, United Kingdom

For details of our global editorial offices, for customer services and for information about how to apply for permission to reuse the copyright material in this book please see our website at www.wiley.com.

Wiley publishes in a variety of print and electronic formats and by print-on-demand. Some material included with standard print versions of this book may not be included in e-books or in print-on-demand. If this book refers to media such as a CD or DVD that is not included in the version you purchased, you may download this material at http://booksupport.wiley.com. For more information about Wiley products, visit www.wiley.com.

Designations used by companies to distinguish their products are often claimed as trademarks. All brand names and product names used in this book and on its cover are trade names, service marks, trademarks or registered trademarks of their respective owners. The publisher and the book are not associated with any product or vendor mentioned in this book. None of the companies referenced within the book have endorsed the book.

Limit of Liability/Disclaimer of Warranty: While the publisher and author have used their best efforts in preparing this book, they make no representations or warranties with respect to the accuracy or completeness of the contents of this book and specifically disclaim any implied warranties of merchantability or fitness for a particular purpose. It is sold on the understanding that the publisher is not engaged in rendering professional services and neither the publisher nor the author shall be liable for damages arising herefrom. If professional advice or other expert assistance is required, the services of a competent professional should be sought.

Library of Congress Cataloging-in-Publication Data is available.

A catalogue record for this book is available from the British Library.

ISBN 978-1-119-27445-2 (hbk)
ISBN 978-1-119-27446-9 (ebk) ISBN 978-1-119-27444-5 (ebk)

Cover design: Wiley

Set in 10/14.5pt PalatinoLTStd by Aptara Inc., New Delhi, India
Printed in Great Britain by TJ International Ltd, Padstow, Cornwall, UK

CONTENTS

INTRODUCTION

'A brand for a company is like a reputation for a person. You earn reputation by trying to do hard things well.'

— Jeff Bezos

The new world of reputation

Not so long ago, your circle of influence went as far as you could see. Your reputation extended to people who could physically see you. Contact was frequent and guaranteed. If you did a good job at work, you could easily control what people thought about you.

This was your 'hallway' reputation. People stuck around. Job change was rare. People had a chance to get to know you over an extended period of time. You gained influence gradually and got promoted because you lasted the course.

Now you find yourself in a new world of new rules. The online space means you have to deal with social media, instant news and frightening transparency. Barriers have fallen between countries, cultures and boundaries. Globalization has levelled the playing field. Workforces are much more diverse – multicultural and multilingual.

We live in complex, uncertain, but exciting times. Mobile phones and digital technology give even average people the chance to build a brand around themselves. Anyone can own a business, write a blog and send an opinion round the world. Attention spans have fallen, marketing messages have exploded and noise has increased dramatically.

Jobs for life are rare. Who gets offered tenure these days? Who even wants it? People want passion, freedom, significance and choice. Of course, that's all still there, but there are millions of people looking for it. Which means predatory competition and a brutal, unstable job market. How will you compete?

This book maintains that the ability to market yourself, create career capital and build reputational stock are what will give you the edge that gets you chosen. Your 'in person' and your 'online' reputation are both at stake. If cultivated properly, together they could be your most valuable commercial asset.

A quick definition of terms

Let's get clear on a few key terms before you press on. You'll see these throughout the book.

- **Your job**. What you do every day. It's your job title, your role, your position. What's on your business card. It's what brings the money in. It's what happens between your commutes.
- **Your work**. It's what you do in your job. It's your contribution or why people actually pay you. You swap your skills, expertise, time and labour for a wage. And if you're lucky, they throw in a few other benefits, like pension, flexible working or healthcare.
- **Your career**. Your path towards more meaningful work or a better job. It's your roadmap of increasingly better opportunities and positions. It's your route to more choice, autonomy and freedom in your working life.

- **Your reputation**. What people say about you behind your back. It's your good name. It's a blend of four things:
  1. your professional capabilities and 'on the job' performance
  2. your profile and visibility with the people that count
  3. your positioning and perceived authority in the minds of people that count and
  4. your PBA (Personal Board of Advisors) and the leverage, advocacy and support they bring to your efforts.

Keep these in mind as you journey through the new world of work, leadership and career management.

Your career playbook for a life of fulfilment

This playbook will propel you quickly to the top of your tree. Or at least more quickly along a meaningful and enjoyable career path. If you're already at the top, this is about keeping you there with more control, influence, recognition and engagement. If you're already in a role you love, it's about keeping you there too, with more security, more control and more flexibility. It's about freedom to choose.

This is your fast-track guide to boardroom opportunities, recognition of your brilliance, backing of your potential, investment in your ideas and engagement with your vision. It's a guide to intrapreneurship or how to think and act like an entrepreneur in order to thrive within the constraints of a big corporation or firm.

These things rarely happen by accident or good fortune. That's why this playbook is packed with a ton of practical ways for you to hit your career and leadership goals intentionally and faster. It's not a theoretical work and it's not grounded in a master's thesis or academic research. It's a pragmatic guide that gives you a variety of ways to become the number one obvious choice for what you do. *Jim L*

It's a career playbook for a life of fulfilment. Sounds a bit grand, but your work probably defines you. If your work is good, you're probably a happy bunny. When people ask you who you are or what you do, you'll probably lead with your job title or the industry you're in. So it's a 'how to' manual for controlling your career and securing work you love on your terms.

This is also aimed at leaders, whether thought leaders or business leaders. I'm calling you a leader since you're probably already in the top 5% of brains and talent in the world right now. After all, you're reading this book! And with this kind of power, you're an influencer and a change agent. That means you're already some kind of leader.

Finally, this book is a time machine. Sure, you'll make it to where you want to be in your career. This will just get you there faster. It's a fast-track mechanism for career progression. The vehicle that will propel you there is called 'career capital' and the key to the car is called reputation.

Although intangible, reputation has a value. And if it has a value, then it also has a cost. *Reward and risk.* Your reputation will take you a long time to build and a moment to ruin. But you can accelerate the building process by intentionally and purposefully doing good things that enhance your good name. After that, it's a case of marketing yourself well enough that good people talk about it. You're a brand, and all brands make good promises and need good promotion.

Problems this book may solve for you

Listen, if you've ever …

- wondered how to move quickly up the ladder in a big firm, large organization or competitive industry
- watched others get the credit for your ideas

- been overlooked for a project, promotion or opportunity
- struggled for job satisfaction, meaning and fulfilment
- found it hard to convert your talent and potential into tangible career progression
- been frustrated that people don't quite get you, or don't see your brilliance
- failed to make an impact at a key moment
- felt restricted by the control others have over your working conditions
- worked really hard for little or no recognition
- thought people above you are not as good as you
- feared for your job in tough economic times
- been paralysed by too many career choices or job options

… then it's almost certain that this book will help you hugely. It's your playbook to quickly and strategically navigate through the career gears to a higher and higher calling. It will show you how to play the Career Game that most people don't even know they're in. It will show you how to create the necessary personal reputation that will cut through the crap and open the doors to the best jobs and opportunities. Creating a good name and a powerful reputation as a 'go-to' guy or girl is going to further your cause.

You're about to get the low down on how to connect at high levels for valuable advocacy, influence and sponsorship. You're going to learn the dimensions of executive presence – that boardroom gravitas that shows you're a peer of the senior players. And you're going to create a game plan of powerful reputation-building strategies that play to your unique strengths, personality and objectives.

This book in a nutshell

You may not have seen your reputation as a career weapon or leadership platform before now. But you're holding this career playbook and you feel there's something in it. It makes sense then for you to know exactly what your reputation is and how it works for or against you.

So, in the first part of the book, we'll define reputation properly and make the strongest case for its relevance to your career and business success. You'll get clarity over the difference between your personal brand and your reputation, and even what role your character plays in all that. Then you'll discover how the *unholy trinity* of online, mobile and digital have changed the way your reputation is built and broken.

You'll quickly see that as a leader and influencer (which you are, no matter what you might think) your reputation is an intangible yet critical career asset. In fact, the higher up you go, the more your personal reputation can make or break the people and company you represent. Then we get to the 'meat' of the book …

The four reputational toolboxes

The second half of this book is the real 'how to' stuff. The nuts and bolts. The specific strategies you can deploy in building your own great name and store of career capital. The way you do it will be different to the way everybody else does it. That's why there are so many strategies to choose from.

Your mission as you read this book is to apply yourself to making it work for you and you alone. What works for you won't necessarily work for your colleague. You've got to play the game with your strengths, your weapons, your game plan. Everyone is different, but the general principles of 'be remarkable, market yourself well and trade smartly' apply to all.

The reputation vault

Everything you need is in this book. Probably. But who knows? You could be one of those hungry people who really get it and want more. You could be a fascinated student of the topic in need of supplementary materials. You could have bigger plans for your reputation than I thought.

That's why you've got the Reputation Vault. It's a hidden resource just for people who have bought the book. You get a bunch of useful worksheets, manifestos and interviews that wouldn't fit into the book. Not because they weren't worthy or instructive. But because there was not enough room.

For instance, the Executive Presence Manifesto does a deep dive into that subtle blend of gravitas, temperament, inner strength, credibility, charisma and skills that gets you viewed as a player and a peer of the top people. Resources like this supplement the book and ground you in the methodology.

You've got unrestricted access to the Vault with our compliments. Go to www.Rep.NetworkingCoachingAcademy.com/repvault and put in the access details supplied in the Additional Resources section at the back of the book.

For now, focus on what you have right here. Forget about the Vault for the moment. Let's just ensure you get the very most out of this book …

Part One

Laying the Foundations

'More than a great database, a killer product or service, a set of skills, or a particular talent – your reputation is the single biggest factor in whether or not you will be a success on this planet.'

– Rob Brown

Chapter 1

Why Build Your Reputation?

'Life is for one generation. A good name is forever.'
— Japanese proverb

One of the lucky ones

Some people are lucky when it comes to career progression. They seem to fall on their feet and into the 'plum' jobs with huge salaries and massive influence. People say good things about them. They attract the endorsement of influential people. They lead committed, enthusiastic followers. They seem to know and are known by all the right people for all the right reasons.

These people get offered the best positions on the best terms. If they want international travel and an exotic life abroad, they get that. If they want a flexible schedule, an ideal job based in their home town so they can enjoy a great family life, that kind of autonomy seems to be available to them. If they want to lead a team, community or project, they quickly find themselves in charge.

They shoot up the career ladder and end up quickly in key leadership positions. More annoyingly, they somehow end up doing the really enjoyable, fun and interesting stuff. They love their job and they love their life. And you hate them.

How did all this happen? Obviously these people prospered because they were in the right place at the right time, right? They just got lucky. They're not better than you. They might even be a whole lot worse. They just got the breaks. Or did they?

Success like this is rarely an accident. These are Career Pros. They've always known something you don't. They've networked their way to the top. They've developed a substantial reputation and huge social capital to get them where they are.

The good news is that if they did it, so can you. With very few exceptions, the career approach or success system of the high flyers and influential, respected leaders is duplicable.

Your stagnation or frustration has been because you've never known quite how to replicate that. Until now, that is. Because now you've got the playbook for career acceleration and job fulfilment. And it's all wrapped up in your good name, your personal brand and your reputation.

What exactly is a reputation?

Your reputation is simply the impression that others have of you. You should value it, protect it, shape it and grow it. Done right, it could give you a significant competitive advantage in your career. Your career counts, because it gives you the platform, autonomy and influence to change the world.

Your current reputation may be good, bad or indifferent. But you've got one. If you look up reputation in any good dictionary, you'll find things like this:

1. The general estimation in which a person is held by the public.
2. The state or situation of being held in high esteem.
3. The general opinion of the public towards a person, a group of people or an organization.

4. Your overall quality or character as seen or judged by people in general.
5. The perception of you and your name in society.

Ultimately, your reputation is what people say, think and feel about you behind your back. It's the degree to which you are held in high esteem (or otherwise) by others. When all that's left of you is your business card or your last blog post, it's the memory, the impact and the impression you leave behind. Here's my definition.

'Your reputation is what influences people to think, feel and talk about you the way they do.'

The reason everyone pays

Your reputation wins you popularity contests. It makes people choose you and what you do. It makes them hire you or fire you. It's your REP – the Reason Everyone Pays. What exactly do you want people to pay? Three things:

1. **Respect**. A solid reputation encourages people to treat you as a partner and peer rather than worker or commodity. They'll promote you and defend you. They pay you a fair price for what you do, don't haggle and refer you to others.
2. **Attention**. In today's crowded, competitive marketplace, the challenge for you is to stand out just enough to get chosen. A formidable reputation will do that for you. It cuts through the clutter, the rhetoric and the noise so that people notice you more than everyone else.
3. **Money**. A solid reputation makes you desirable, hirable and promotable. All of which means more control, more choices and more money. You might do what you do JUST for the love of it, but I doubt it. Highly reputed individuals can always leverage their status for premium rates, maximum choice and ultimate autonomy. If they

want to build a platform and a following, they will. And because they resolve problems and pain for their followers, they'll make money. Money usually follows pain.

If you want people to pay you respect, attention and money, you're going to need a decent reputation that sets you apart from the pack.

You already have a reputation

Whether you realize it or not, you probably already have a reputation. Whether it's a good one or not, we're not sure yet. The truth is, you probably don't know exactly what your reputation is or what you did to get it. But it's likely you've got one.

You don't have to be famous to have a reputation. Reputation isn't reserved for high-profile leaders or thinkers. It's simply the perception owned by others of who you are and what you do. So if you're appearing on the radars of anyone, they're now making decisions about you.

Your reputation could be neutral, weak and inconsequential, which is bad. When people don't know you (or of you), then you're irrelevant. You don't factor into their hiring decisions. They're not hanging on your words. They don't care.

Your reputation could be negative and inhibitive. This is worse than bad. When people perceive you badly or wrongly, your efforts to get on and get ahead will be severely hampered. This reputation may or may not be of your own making. But you'll need to overturn and overcome it if you're going to get things back on track.

Your reputation could be strong and positive. People speak well of you. Life and work are a whole lot easier. You get perks, favours and shortcuts. Opportunities open up for you. Good things happen to you.

Your name and personal brand are powerful weapons in the corporate career battle. The decision to promote you to partner or the boardroom will be taken when you're not in the room. Your credentials as a leader of people or thinking come down to the power of your name. When you control that, you control your world.

The dangers of a poor (or no) reputation

A bad reputation will kill you. You'll struggle in your career, which will adversely affect your personal life. You'll take on roles and jobs because you have to, not because you want to. You'll find yourself in the despicable position of fulfilling other people's dreams and achieving other people's goals.

A poor reputation means you'll struggle to earn what you're worth. You'll find it hard to secure a job you enjoy in a place you like living with people you enjoy the company of. You'll get frustrated by a lack of voice, a shaky platform for your ideas and no engaged following for your thoughts.

You'll be at risk when you put forward good ideas and suggestions. Your credibility will suffer and people won't take you seriously. It can take you years to eradicate the effects of a poor reputation. People seem to have long memories. Records go back a long way. Stuff online never seems to go away.

It's similar when you have no reputation. Google yourself and see what comes up. If it's nothing on the first couple of pages, you're invisible. In a void of reputational collateral, people make up their own minds. They distrust. They assume. They ask the wrong people about you. They get a distorted picture. You can't afford to be anonymous.

If you don't build your reputation, others will do it for you. If you don't claim that authority space, somebody else will. You can't ignore your reputation. You don't have the luxury of being ignorant of what others think about you. Shape it yourself. Try to own your personal brand.

There are some suggestions later in the book to help rebuild or restore a broken or bad reputation. The best strategy, though, is to build it true and strong in the first place, and guard it with everything you've got.

Ten big benefits of a stand-out reputation

Your reputation is your personal share price on the stock market of life. It dictates how much people will invest in you. It's your most valuable career asset. It says the people that count should choose you and nobody else.

Your reputation defines how people perceive you. It propels you into positions of leadership and influence. It gives you meaningful work and interesting projects. It lends credibility to your ideas and your inventions.

A good reputation as any kind of high performer, influencer, player, expert, authority or contributor in your space gives you the following 10 benefits.

1. **Stand-out status**. You're not alone. You have competition for openings, placements, projects, places, promotions, deals, mentors, funding, backing, endorsements, sponsorship, perks, privileges. Can you rise above the noise to claim your prize?
2. **Media attention**. Reporters need experts. Journalists require facts, insight, quotations and opinions from people in the know. Media interest seeks out those well-reputed authority figures.
3. **Influence**. Your good name and expert status will make people take action. People are naturally conditioned to respect authority figures. That means people will pay attention to you and what you stand for. They will hunt you down as the ultimate source,

because nobody else will do. That's when you can sell your ideas, your case for promotion and your contribution.

4. **Strategic alliances**. People want to partner with you when you're somebody of significance. They want your ideas, your influence, your endorsement and will want to collaborate with you. This in turn opens you up to new audiences and opportunities.

5. **Prestige and popularity**. In every buying or hiring decision, every-one wants the best. Gold medal, not silver. Top prize, not second. As a stand-out performer, authority or expert, you gain prestige and popularity. People will revere you and rave about you. They will chase you and want to work with you. People admire and share your 'art'. They spread your messages and are privileged to do so. They recommend you to their contacts, friends and lists. Reputation gets you on the podium in life's many popularity contests.

6. **Premium rates**. People with the best reputations and expert authority status have the most control and the strongest bargain-ing chip in negotiations. They usually earn more and seem worth more.

7. **Satisfaction and fulfilment**. With a good reputation comes choice. Choice to do more significant, enjoyable and fulfilling work. Choice to work where and how you want. Choice to wear or not wear a tie. You get the idea.

8. **Protection and forgiveness**. If your reputation is good, people will guard your actions. They'll back you up and defend you when you're attacked. When you mess up, they'll forgive you and give you the benefit of the doubt.

9. **Open doors**. When your reputation works for you, marketing yourself and your ideas is so much easier. It takes less effort. You gain acceptance and buy-in so much more quickly because of who people think you are – rather than 'I don't know you', they think 'I can't live without you'. Doors open before you that

would otherwise be closed. People will buy you, saying 'where do I sign?' instead of 'who are you?'

10. **When you build a formidable reputation, interesting things happen to you**. Good things. You'll naturally attract influence and connections. You'll gain valuable career opportunities. Life somehow becomes easier and more fun.

Your good name goes before you in ensuring that the best deals, opportunities, promotions and projects come to you instead of your competition. It makes you more and more indispensable.

You might not ultimately land that dream job or carve out that perfect career. But by cultivating your value and your reputation, you increase the chances that it will happen. With all these massive upsides, your reputation is worth investing in and guarding. This book shows you exactly how.

Reputation is the ultimate social proof

The power of social proof is immense. Robert Cialdini's seminal work *Influence: The Psychology of Persuasion* blew the lid on the power of how people make choices based on what others do and say. You are a social animal. You are influenced and conditioned by other people around you. This is sometimes called the herd mentality.

If one person follows you, others will follow them following you. It just takes one fanatic to start a movement, and one dedicated follower to kickstart a campaign for your election. But it takes a multitude to get you noticed. A crowd is usually louder than a lone voice.

If you get approval, good word of mouth or endorsements from influential people, it boosts your reputation. If you get your thoughts and ideas shared and read by peers and followers, your reputation grows. All because people watch what other people do, and then do the same. They assume those people or influencers know what they are doing, and they copy.

It's an accepted fact that what buyers say about a product or service affects people's purchasing decisions. This includes customer testimonials, case studies and online reviews. The word from our peers is much more trusted than product descriptions from manufacturers. Some other examples of social proof in action:

- Restaurants and bars with full tables. People assume the food is good and the place is popular. Same with queues or lines outside night clubs or at fairground rides.
- The frenzy for concert tickets, both online and waiting in line.
- Online reviews for mobile apps, books, vacations and movies.
- TV shows using 'canned laughter' or recorded applause to make you laugh and clap.

When others say you're great, word gets around. You're good because others say you are. That's how viral videos and word of mouth works. People share stuff all the time. Now more than ever. Good and especially bad. Give them good things to say and report on, and your reputation is now being shaped for the better.

The nine unbreakable rules of reputation

People have tried to break the following rules of reputation. And failed.

1. **You can't totally control your reputation**. You can influence it but not 100% control it.
2. **Reputation is not a quick fix**. It's a long-term game, not a short-term play.

3. **Reputation is not fame**. Just because you're famous doesn't mean your reputation is good.
4. **Your reputation will be attacked**. The higher up you go, the more you'll get shot at.
5. **Perception beats reality**. No matter what's real, it's what people think that counts.
6. **Lack of scandal does not mean a good reputation**. Not getting it wrong is not getting it right.
7. **Everything is in the public domain**. There are no secrets. It's all out there one way or another.
8. **You can have multiple reputations**. Different situations, different people, different perceptions.
9. **Invisibility is not an option**. If you don't define your reputation, others will do it for you.

Let's deep dive these so you're fully aware of how they all work for you and against you.

Rule 1: You can't totally control your reputation

You're an ambassador of your company's reputation and the guardian of your own personal reputation. As a leader, influencer and rising star this should be easy. You're a master of control, right? You haven't got where you are today without having some control over people, messages, direction.

Alas, you have less control over your reputation than you'd like. It's like beauty – it's in the eye of the beholder. People are fickle, flakey, opinionated, complicated and emotional. You can't force people to like you and trust you.

You have a certain amount of control over personal brand. You can monitor what appears out there to some degree. Even the stuff you're not in total control of. You probably have no say in how your business card or company website looks. You may have restrictions on using social media or what's allowed on your LinkedIn profile.

Once your personal brand, your ideas and your work are out there, it's largely out of your hands. You can't easily control how people will perceive it. You can hope they'll like it and they'll dig you. But you can't make people love you.

Some people will love you for wearing a tie or looking smart. Some people will hate you for it. Once you let the arrow fly, you can't influence 100% where or how it lands. You'll never please everyone and, actually, you shouldn't want to. Just the people that count.

The key is to create the best possible version of you, your work and your character. Then promote it to the best possible people who make the most critical decisions about your future. That's the smart way to play and win with your career.

Rule 2: Reputation is not a quick fix

In the world of work and business, your 'go-to' status won't happen overnight. It won't even happen by chance. You're building a platform here. A house if you like. Brick by brick. Comment by comment. Conversation by conversation. Even if you could build it fast, how sturdy would it be? How robust in repelling the changing winds of public opinion? How flexible in surviving the changing allegiances or strategies of hiring individuals? How vigorous in coping with the rapid changes in technology and trends?

You don't want to be a one-hit wonder. Any fool can get hired or booked once. The best, most sought-after thought leaders and prime promotional candidates didn't start out yesterday. It's a slog. It means some heavy lifting. It's going to take a little time. And it's going to be so worth it!

There's nothing wrong with legitimately cutting some corners to get there faster. But be under no illusions, building a great reputation requires a consistent, focused effort. Tortoise and the hare. Slow and steady wins the race. Marathon, not a sprint, and all that. With a few spurts here and there.

Rule 3: Reputation is not celebrity

If I offered you a million followers on Twitter, instantly, would you take them? Probably yes. After all, you'd be seen as popular, because perception is reality, right? If people see that you're popular, and believe that you're popular, then a million people can't be wrong. Ergo, you're good.

But think about it. What if those 1million followers were dead accounts, dummy profiles or just robots? Okay, what if they were real people but had absolutely no interest in or relevance to what you do? They don't work in your world or live in your country. They don't like what you like, do what you do or care what you think. They wouldn't read your tweets, respect your opinions or share your ideas. Do you still want them?

Look, you're not a celebrity here. You're not famous. You probably don't want to be if you've got your degree and gone into corporate life. Only professionals with very big egos do 'fame'. That's probably not you. If it was, you'd be on some talent reality show, playing in a rock band or following some risky, world-changing entrepreneurial path.

Celebrity is quick fix. Overnight success. Art. Fame. Adulation. Some of that is alright, but let's get real. You're building a career. Brick by brick. Conversation by conversation. Word by word. You're climbing the ladder. Nobody will give you the top job no matter how good your MBA is or what school you went to. You've got to earn it. Practise your craft. Build up your career capital. Be so good they can't ignore you.

Rule 4: Your reputation will be attacked

There are too many examples of well-known people who have felt impregnable, only to be toppled. When you make a name for yourself, you'll make enemies. People will be jealous of what you're doing. For some rivals, you're in their way. You stand between them and their goals.

Career management can be adversarial. Brutal even. Lazy people will despise your efforts. Corrupt people will fear your integrity. Good people will be jealous of your greatness. Safe people will be distrustful of your risk-taking. Shy people will be suspicious of your self-promotion.

You won't win over everyone. You're not immune to a crisis. And you WILL be attacked. When that happens, you'll hopefully be robust enough to withstand it. Your advocates will hopefully be loud enough in number and influence to fight your corner. You will hopefully be in a strong position to ignore (as one swats away a fly) or refute (as one confronts a liar). Just be ready.

Rule 5: Perception = Reality

What people see, think, do, feel and say when they come into contact with you, your name or your 'art' counts more than what's real about you. Change the perception and you change the reality. It's not enough to be the best. You have to *be seen to be the best.* What people think and see is what really counts, not what is actually the case.

If they think you're unreliable, you're unreliable. Even if you're really not. You may not know that they think you're unreliable, nor WHY they think you're unreliable. Because they believe it makes it so. Your goal in building and managing your reputation then becomes to give people as much reason as possible to think and believe the right things about you.

The good news is that you can influence how others perceive you and thus your empire. You can't really control it, since they'll think what they think.

But your strategy is to give them so much good stuff to talk about, they don't see any bad stuff.

In that regard, you can craft your personal reputation. There are a small number of leaders in every industry or profession who do just that. They are the 'stand-out' key people of influence. Almost everybody knows them, rates them and raves about them. They are the obvious choice and trusted voice.

These beacons of influence are often no better than anyone else. But they are perceived so by their staff, peers, tribe, fans, followers and stakeholders. Regardless of any personal standards you hold yourself to, being seen to do and say the right thing is mostly what makes your reputation.

Make the strongest possible case for your brilliance and authority. This makes it hard for people to misinterpret. Create an abundance of good stuff that outweighs any bad stuff. Monitor and manage the conversation. Perceptions can change and where yours are negative, your job is to change them for the better.

Rule 6: Lack of scandal does not mean a good reputation

A good reputation doesn't happen by NOT doing bad things. In a celebrity-obsessed culture, personalities lead the news. We are fascinated less by companies than by the people who lead and work for them. A tenacious media, a hungry public and a good story are a potent combination.

Some people try a 'head down and keep quiet' approach. People mistakenly think that if they 'keep their nose clean' and do a good job, they'll get promoted. Not true. You may stay out of trouble, but you're doing nothing to make your case for advancement.

You could be working in an immoral, corrupt environment. One where merely staying out of the limelight constitutes virtue. Get out of there and get building a serious reputation for making a positive difference.

Just by being average or mediocre, you certainly beat the useless and the lousy. By doing nothing, you can beat the person who does a bad something. You can do better than that though. Your standards are too low. The keyword is BUILD a good reputation. Not HOPE one comes to you by default.

Rule 7: Everything is in the public domain

Deciding how information appears in public is a fine line between control and transparency. That's why PR departments and media experts are paid huge sums to ensure the good stuff is shared and the bad stuff is buried.

Be transparent. Everything finds a way to get out eventually. There are no secrets. Everything is visible. The new world of internet, digital and mobile means *leakage* is both inevitable and instant. You can't control what gets out there.

What happens in the boardroom often doesn't stay in the boardroom. Emails sent, phone calls made and private conversations conducted all too often become public domain. Despite what you might want to keep behind closed doors, much can be found out, particularly if it is deemed to be in the public interest.

You have control over much but not all of your world. Private thoughts quickly become public perceptions. Emails aren't private. Think twice before you hit 'send'. Conversations aren't 100% private. Meetings aren't 100% secluded.

Deleted files aren't gone. They're on your system somewhere. Be careful about what you say online and on social media. It may stay there forever. People can take screenshots of stuff you post so it's permanent even when you take it down.

Think ahead on your actions. Some hustle and risk-taking is all well and good. But make it strategic and calculated. It all ends up in the public domain. Everyone is an amateur detective. Stuff gets found out. Keep your nose clean.

Rule 8: You can have multiple reputations

You can't be good at everything and you can't be popular with everyone. Your reputation in your community or neighbourhood might be different to your work. What people think about you at your church, mosque or synagogue may be very different to how you're viewed at home. Your online persona could be unrecognizable to your hallway (face-to-face) reputation.

Your reputation for certain activities will vary. You'll have a reputation for the way you drive and the way you do DIY projects. One for speaking in public and one for listening in private. Reputation is also situational. It depends where you are, what you're doing and who your stakeholders are.

Reputation is sometimes like self-esteem (what you think about yourself). Your overall self-esteem is made up of lots of little self-esteems (the way you think you drive, talk, walk, present and network). Your overall reputation is made up of how people see you in different situations doing different things. Your aim is to be congruent. To be consistent across situations, audiences and platforms.

Rule 9: Invisibility is not an option

Anonymity is not the answer. Sticking your head in the sand and pretending that the internet doesn't exist is impossible. Even if you accept the power of the internet, it's inconceivable that you could be invisible or 'unfindable' online.

I like the joke by Lori Randall Stradtman, author of *Online Reputation Management For Dummies*. 'Where's the best place to hide a dead body? On page 3 of Google's search results.'

Of course, *it's still on Google*, even if few people are looking. And it's permanent! Personal branding expert William Arruda goes further. 'If you don't show up in a Google search of your name, you don't exist.'

Bottom line, if you're not researchable, you'll be neglected and forgotten. You'll be viewed as irrelevant and even suspicious. If they can't be bothered to dig, that's usually not a good sign. It means you don't really matter.

If you want what you do to count, yet you don't give people the evidence for your brilliance, then you're leaving a black hole of reputational collateral. What people can't find, they make up or decide for themselves.

The importance of reputation for leaders

Few people in positions of influence and responsibility (henceforth leaders) give much attention to their own personal brand and personal reputation. Yet as a leader, you are the guardian and ambassador of whatever and whoever you lead.

This applies to your company or your community. The corporate reputation stands and falls on the personal reputation of its people and particularly its leader. You drive the brand, set the culture and model the values. As a leader, your personal reputation is inseparable from that of your company.

More dangerously, your good name is often shaped by the media and the public. If you don't give it to them, somebody else will. And if nobody else will, they have the means to find it out. Julian Assange, founder of online site Wiki Leaks, has made a career out of insider knowledge – exposing scandal, cover-up and conspiracy.

You're unlikely to be next, but a decent hacker could probably find your bank account details, passwords and your web browsing history in a few seconds. How would that play out in the public domain?

If you get a moment, Google *Playing to Win in the Reputation Economy*, a study of leaders by The Reputation Institute. They surveyed 301 business leaders across 28 industries and 29 countries and found that 78% acknowledged they were living in a new world where who you are as an individual is directly tied to company success.

> 'The world and your operating environment has become more complex. More stakeholders care about you ... they want to know who the ... people behind the brands are. They have access to mission-critical information about you 24/7 and can disrupt your strategy with a single click or bad review.'

You don't even need to be at the top of the food chain to get it in the neck. The report goes on: 'But who does the CEO call when they want to know where the reputation risk lies across key stakeholders in your largest markets ... YOU!'

Career success means reputational scrutiny

We're in the Information Age or Knowledge Economy. Your empire is not just bricks and mortar. Its value comes from hard to define stuff like engagement, talent, relationships, culture and innovation. You play a part in that. Your personal share price on the stock market of life dictates what people are willing to pay for you and invest in you. Your reputation matters.

What people know, think and say about you matters. Your reputation is out there. It's in the hands of your stakeholders, your peers and the people in your empire. The higher up you go, the more your personal reputation can make or break your career and even the company you work for. Your personal reputation is inextricably linked to that of your company. You represent them on the public stage.

As you go higher, you also encounter more reputational scrutiny. Your narrative becomes public interest. Your good name will get you through doors, which is good. At the same time, your own personal reputation becomes inextricably linked to everyone and everything you represent.

As a leader, you are an influencer and change agent. Much of what you do, think and say plays out across communities and online platforms. There are few secrets and almost total transparency. What you say and do, your personal standing and your good name – it all helps promote the company's brand. It affects public trust in the company's activities.

What people know and say about you can be good 'coin' for you. As long as they don't use it against you, in which case it's going to cost you a small fortune to make it go away. Knowledge, and thus reputation, is currency. Earn it well and trade it wisely.

Everybody is a leader and an influencer

If you're thinking you're not really a leader and that your personal reputation has no bearing on the corporate one, think again. It's said that even the most introverted person in the world will influence thousands of people in their lifetime. This is good news and bad. It gives you power and significance. It also gives you responsibility and accountability.

It's not just the people at the top who lead. If you're in charge of just one person, you're a leader. If you have a say in the life of just one other human being, you're a leader. If you run a team, a project or a campaign you're a leader. If you head up a department, a division, a country or a region, you're a leader.

If you're still arguing this, you want to be a leader, right? You've got plans and ideas you think could make a difference. You've got a significant contribution to make. You're not just here to make up the numbers. To give you the freedom, the power and the platform to do that, you must be out front. Inspiring people. Doing the stuff you do best. Building a great profile.

Your career is at stake and to have maximum control, you're going to need all the leadership and influencing skills you can muster.

Your reputation drives company success

When business leaders are asked about the tangible benefits of a good personal and corporate reputation, four wins come up:

1. Drives competitive differentiation.
2. Attracts and retains top talent.
3. Allows better collaboration and partnership with key opinion leaders and policy makers.
4. Enables better crisis management.

In an article entitled 'Connecting Marketing Metrics to Financial Consequences', Wharton Professor David Reibstein pointed to studies showing that 50% of corporations' value today is composed of intangible assets (such as intellectual property, customer loyalty, reputation and relationships), up from just 20% 40 years ago. And it is primarily these intangibles, not hard assets, that dictate a company's valuation by the stock market.

Personal and corporate reputation is a bottom line discussion. When leaders take it seriously, they are given the leeway to try new things and take risks. They buy some forgiveness, inoculation and time if things don't go so well.

Your good name goes a long way. It's worth looking after. Let's get you in the game and embark you on the journey of an irresistible personal reputation that will open big career doors into even bigger opportunities!

Says the same thing on repeat (handwritten annotation)

When leaders get reputation wrong

Your reputation is in many ways the most valuable thing you own. It can take years to build and be destroyed in an instant. You only need to look at the PR gaffes and howlers throughout history to see how fragile a reputation can be. This is especially so when the 'brand' is a person rather than a company.

As a leader, when you *bomb*, the company or empire often goes with you. A glance at the everyday press will show you how the acts and comments of CEOs can affect share price, public trust and employee engagement.

Sometimes an off-the-cuff remark can bring down an empire. Ask Gerald Ratner, once a leading English jeweller who sank his company overnight with an inopportune comment. When asked how he can sell his jewellery for such a low price, he replied *'Because it's total crap'*. His words were instantly seized upon by the media and an estimated £500m was wiped from the value of the company.

Sometimes PR gaffes are worse than the original crisis. Ask Tony Hayward, former CEO of oil and energy company BP. He emerged as the public face of the oil giant and was crucified in the press for how he handled a huge oil spill in the Gulf in 2010. He was derided for his flippant and insensitive remarks in media interviews such as *'I'd like my life back'* and *'The spill is relatively tiny in comparison with the size of the ocean'*.

Hayward's credibility was shot. By the time he was replaced the following year, the company had lost almost a quarter of its market value and had haemorrhaged over $40 billion in costs associated with clean-up and recovery.

Even if you're not to blame or had no idea what was happening on your watch, leaders still have to take the fall. How leaders handle PR problems that are not even of their making can make or break both their own and their company's reputations. Ask Martin Winterkorn, former CEO of Volkswagen, Audi and Porsche.

Winterkorn resigned in 2015 after an emissions cheating scandal with the company's diesel cars. He won't be short of money. *Forbes* business magazine recently rated him the 58th most powerful person. But his reputation will forever be tarnished by what happened on his watch.

Responsibility travels upwards and, sooner or later, the person at the top will have to answer to someone. The buck gets passed upwards, and if you're not equipped to handle any kind of scrutiny, you'll whither under the kind of grilling that Tony Hayward got. You can quickly become the story and do more damage than the original problem.

Thus, reputation is a double-edged sword. It can be good or evil, beneficial or hindering. When you win, those around you reap the rewards. It will bring you fame or infamy. It will make or break you. And it's not even the truth that matters. People's perceptions often trump the truth.

Face it, what counts as remarkable these days is not expected growth, a reasonably successful brand or your regular season wins. Yesterday's good is tomorrow's great. What wowed people last year is average now. The headlines demand something more dramatic. Your stakeholders want you to come up with something exciting. When you build your reputation in a strategic, focused way, you'll give them that.

Summary – Why you should build your reputation

You are an ambassador for your organization. In a noisy, time-poor, crowded, attention-scarce world, it's the people, not the company, that make the stories. People bring companies to life. They personify the company. The values and vision become synonymous.

When all is well, your high public profile will be a valuable asset for you personally and your employer corporately. When the boat tips and things get tough, what counted for your good may now go against you.

One woman at a large London investment house began developing a high profile during a series of takeovers. She courted it and created some good PR as a result. But when a deal went wrong, the press knew who she was. Her fame became a liability in those difficult times. She recovered and learned.

As you move up the ladder, your personal and public share price goes up. Engagement in your ideas goes up. Buy-in for your initiatives and projects goes up. Loyalty and advocacy goes up. Forgiveness and tolerance for your wrongs goes up.

Your control of people and situations goes up. Confidence in your abilities and your vision goes up. The speed at which you can get things done goes up. Trust in your words and your opinions goes up. Ultimately, your ability to effect change and make a difference is accelerated.

A stand-out reputation lowers resistance to your arguments and excuses. Delay on decisions affecting you goes down. Suspicion and distrust of your motives goes down. Justifications for your ideas and fighting for your strategic position goes down.

Walls, obstacles and barriers come down. Your detractors, saboteurs and nay-sayers melt into obscurity as they lose ground fighting against the swell of positive public opinion. You can see it's a lot more than just increasing your employability.

So now you know exactly what a reputation is and what a good one will do for you. We just need to set the scene for what you're going to do with it. That is, how to play and win the Career Game. Then you're ready to start building a formidable 'go-to' reputation for what you do. One that will make you unstoppable AND give you maximum control and choice in securing the work you love on your terms.

Chapter 2

Setting The Scene – The Career Game

'You can't build a reputation on what you are going to do.'
– Henry Ford

Your primary objective – work on your terms

Your job and your work are a big part of your identity. What you do is who you are. Of course, you may be a parent, a friend and a whole load of other things. But work is important to you. It gives you meaning and fuels your lifestyle.

Being largely defined by your career and your job can be bad news if you lack choice and control. In other words, you're doing the job you have to rather than the work you want to. This book will help you achieve what should be your primary objective – work on your terms.

You're going to see that not everyone gets to choose what they want to do. Actually very few people even *know* what they want to do. This makes them even more frustrated and unhappy. If you'd like to have a say in your career, a stand-out reputation is going to be your biggest and best weapon.

Whether you realize it or not, you're in a game. How you play it will dictate the power and satisfaction you have with your life and career. In this book, you'll discover exactly what this game is and how it's played. You'll learn how you win and also how you lose.

You'll see that intangible collateral like your reputation and your connections are valuable weapons or commodities in this game. Without them, you're forced to feed off the employment scraps that others give you. You're obliged to take the job you have to, not the job you want to. If you don't want that, you must play to win. Winning means securing work on your terms.

The components of 'work on your terms'

While the perfect job or career is so very subjective, let's assume this; that the objective in corporate or professional life is to move up and maybe even out. That means promotions into those careers or roles that you're envious of in your current company. You know, those jobs that you think you'd be good at and would really enjoy down the line.

Moving up and out may also mean having the options at some point to launch your own ship and run your own company. That's not going to happen 'just like that'. You're going to need some skills, some track record, some backing and some reputational clout to make that kind of switch.

Work on your terms means landing that perfect job or following that dream career. What does that look like? You're effectively trying to secure work that gives you as many as possible of the following five characteristics.

1. **Choice** – you want the ability to choose work on your terms.
2. **Creativity** – you want work that is engaging, interesting and inspiring.
3. **Impact** – you want work that gives you meaning, significance and influence.
4. **Control** – you want work that gives you flexibility, life balance and autonomy.
5. **Reward** – you want work that compensates you well for your contribution.

How do you go about getting this kind of work? If you applied for such a job or role right now, would you get it? Not without a great CV or résumé.

An impressive track record. A formidable reputation. Without this stuff to trade in return, you'll be rejected and even laughed at. You're not worth it. Yet. You must have something to trade.

Let's see what you can trade for these jobs by looking at the kind of things that make you valuable and give you career capital. Then you can figure out what kind of shape you're in to secure that next job, promotion, position or opening.

Introducing the career game

Life is a game. Work is a game. Success is a game. The *Oxford English Dictionary* defines a game as a form of competitive activity played according to rules. *Webster's* describes a game as a contest played according to rules with the players in direct opposition to each other.

You're in the **Career Game**. The board is the career landscape. The marketplace. The industry you're in. You win if you shape a great career or the job you want. You win if you can do the work you love on your terms.

When you ask someone what a great career looks like, they mostly say things like 'work I can be passionate about' and 'work where I can make a difference' or 'work where I get really rewarded for my contribution'. Do you have this right now? Or is there a greater prize or position you're after?

The Career Game is a trading game. Like Monopoly or Settlers of Catalan or Civilization or Container. Many more are available from the app store. Trading is the action of buying and selling stuff, traditionally products and services, but also intangibles like reputation and connections.

If you don't like games, or you've not got the appetite to play, you might be wondering whether you can opt out. Be a pacifist. 'I'm not fighting.'

You could. You could pack it all in and become a nomad. You could set up your own game and become self-employed. But you're now in a different game. You're competing for clients and customers and attention. That's still a tough one to win. So you've really got no choice. If you're ambitious and want more than you've got work-wise, then you have to play.

A game with no opt-out

You can't opt-out of the Career Game UNLESS you're happy to have your whole work-life dictated by others. On their terms. In their best interests. If you don't play, everyone else carries on playing. You're quickly going to sink to the bottom of the pack. If you don't play, you lose.

Losing looks like redundancy, lack of options, the inability to earn what you are worth. Losing leads to regret, resentment, jealousy and discontent. That FOMO (fear of missing out) feeling that somehow you've been sidestepped when it comes to handing out the spoils of war.

Losing leads to lack of career choice. All you can do is take the job you're given, not have the job you want. If you can get a job. Losing means a lack of fulfilment and the feeling of having 'settled'. Losing yields feelings of having missed out on your dream and not realizing your potential. Losing is not a nice feeling in any game. Bottom line, you can't opt-out. You're all in.

If you want to make partner or boss of your company, you're in a fight. To get that next promotion or a place on that leadership programme, it's winner takes all. It's logical. Not everyone gets these great jobs or careers. There aren't that many of them.

There are lots of jobs available to the masses that don't have the prestige, choice and control you desire. Many are mundane, repetitive and lacking in purpose. You get little control over your working hours, location, commute, package or choice of tasks.

You don't want this. That's why need a ticket to the game. 'In it to win it' is a cliché but in the Career Game, you know it's true. So if you're committed to playing the game, let's get you to the start line.

The object of the career game

Any ambitious career path is by nature adversarial. Not everyone can win. Not everyone can be top dog. Many can do well. Most can enjoy playing. But however you define the prize, only a few can lay their hands on it.

To win the Career Game, you want work on your terms. You want a fulfilling career. A great job. But great jobs are exceptional. They are prized and limited. Few people ever attain the power and satisfaction of a work-life dictated by their own choices and ambitions. Not everyone gets to live out a fulfilling mission. But it's possible. If you win.

Winning looks like career choice, perks and the most interesting projects. Winning means worthwhile work that you love; a mission and a purpose. Winning offers you wealth, significance and influence. Winning gives you security in tough economic times and bad job markets.

Nobody is going to give you career choice, control and meaning by right. Things like wealth, freedom and independence aren't a given. You've got to earn them. Trade something for them. You've got to be worth it. That is how you play the Career Game. You trade your stuff for their stuff.

If you desire control, influence and significance, you've got to become so valuable, worthy and skilled that you earn the right to ask for and get those things.

Without anything to trade with, you lose choice and power. You can't afford that. Make the decision to build your next job and your future career *on purpose*. Give yourself some options. Are you ready to play?

The four players in the career game

The biggest mistake in the Career Game comes if you don't or can't see you're actually in a game. If that's you, you've already lost. Your only strategy to win is luck, since you're doing nothing intentionally to skew the odds in your favour.

You're relying on the goodwill of others. You need their favour and advocacy. You're relying on the timing of circumstances. Being in the right place at the right time. And you're relying on the ineptitude of your fellow competitors. When they screw up or fall short, you're hopefully on hand to pick up the slack.

This ignorant approach is not advised. It's too reactive. You're relying on other people to dictate the speed of your ascension, the rate at which you acquire choice, control and wealth. Perhaps the bitterest pill to swallow in losing is to see other people succeed who are less talented, hardworking and even less nice than you. That bites! It's not fair and it's not right. But unless you're in the game, you can't really compete.

So let's assume you know you're in the game. There are four kinds of people who play the Career Game. Only one of them wins. Which one are you?

The 4 Kinds of Career Builders

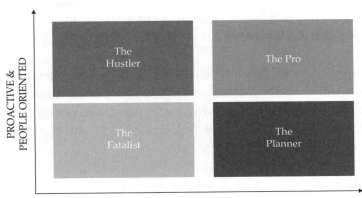

43

1. **The Career Fatalist**. Do you place your career in the hands of the gods? You're kind of aware there's a game going on, but your eternal optimism thinks you'll come out okay. You don't make much effort. You think that promotion, that top job, that great opportunity, will happen just by sticking around. By carrying on doing what you're doing. You're okay with people and you have a vague idea of where you want to go. But that doesn't take you far.

If you are a Career Fatalist, your pitfall is a lack of effort. There are two reasons why you might not be bothered. First is if you have *a sense of entitlement*. If you went to the right school or university, you may feel a glorious career of fulfilling and well-paid work is what you're worth. If you were brought up to expect good things, then not getting what you want will be something of a surprise to you.

You assume that things will work out for you. You look down on the herd. You feel the game is beneath you, and not worthy of you competing. You've fallen on your feet in the past, and you'll do it again. You're not used to failing

The second reason you might show no appetite for the fight is if you're just bone idle. You can't seem to find that drive to get off your ass and do something. You find motivation difficult. You know there's a game but you just don't want to be in it. You perhaps resent having to play at all. It's just, well, too much like hard work.

Either way, you're a Career Fatalist. You wait and see. You leave it to fate – whatever will be will be. But sooner or later, you're going to have to 'show up' and make a contribution of value. You're going to have to get your head in the game. Otherwise you'll get the job you don't want. Maybe even the job nobody wants.

2. **The Career Hustler**. You play hard, fast and loose. You're gutsy and opportunistic. You're also a poor planner and a bad strategist. You get

lucky because you create a lot of your own luck. But you walk through the next door that opens rather than through the right door. You're usually persuasive and very proactive. You're probably a good sales person. But you're not a Career Pro.

If you are a Career Hustler, your pitfall is a lack of strategy. You've got passion and you've got drive. You've even got ideas to change the world, but you've got no game plan. You've got skills and you've got knowledge. You've even got connections. But you've got no strategy to compete and win.

You're maybe even brilliant, driven and well-meaning. But you haven't yet planned the route that will take you to where you want to be.

You're a classic Career Hustler. You exhibit 'ignorance on fire'. Your symptoms are excitement, vision, idealism and optimism. Yet you make success unlikely with no playbook to chart your course. You're aggressive, ad-hoc and spur of the moment. You are people oriented and can light up a room and build armies of connections. You stalk corridors, are socially prolific and seem to be everywhere. You've got chutzpah – you're cheeky, courageous and ballsy. But you suffer from a lack of strategy.

However, there are some people who have a brilliant fool-proof plan and still fail …

3. **The Career Planner**. So you're an amazing strategist. Trouble is you do so much planning, you forget to take action. Or you're so paralysed by the game plan, you don't know exactly how to get moving. You're task focused yet not always good with people. It's this that slows you down.

If this is you, you're a classic Career Planner. You read all the books and do all the psychometric tests. You invest in the coaching and mentoring. You do the online programs. You map it all out. Your résumé or CV is kicking and you look great on paper. You're ultra-focused and super-organized. Yet you fail to take action.

Instead, you dither. You prefer planning to meeting. You go for strategizing over executing. You are busy with social media and you favour networking online over the face-to-face stuff. You love spreadsheets and career quizzes. You're not lazy. In fact, you're very industrious and often very productive. Maybe even creative. But ultimately you become paralysed into inaction.

You end up being timid, anxious and hopeful. Too scared to make a move and too cautious to take a chance. That's why you lose. The hustlers stream past you. Rivals seize the moment before they do. Opportunities come and go. Doors will open and close. And you'll fail to walk through them. Which is a fail.

4. **The Career Pro**. You're purposeful and strategic. You're also opportunistic and random. You understand how luck can play a part as long as you stay open to chance encounters and serendipity.

You want to stand out and are driven to make it happen. You have big career dreams plans and are taking steps to get there. You're focused and determined in your quest to build career capital.

Your reputation is important to you, and you know what currency it creates in the job market. You're hungry to be at the front of the line when they're handing out those dream jobs. You are coachable and ready to invest in yourself to trade up in the Career Game. If this is you, you're holding the playbook to make it all real.

One final word of warning. There are two subtle traps that you can still fall into, even if you are a Career Pro ...

1. The trap of being brilliant but anonymous

You don't really believe that if you do a great job, you'll get noticed, get promoted and be given the keys to career heaven. You're not that naïve. You're reading this book, so you know it's not that easy.

Leading with your work or your output is a dangerous strategy. It will speak for you if it gets heard or noticed. But it won't speak for you quite like you can. For that you need personal marketing and reputation management. You need to position yourself well and raise your profile. Many a light has been hidden under a bushel or bowl. Inadvertently you keep your amazing qualities and your super-hero abilities secret from others.

You don't like to brag, of course. It's all very noble of you. But you're a well-kept secret, and that will not serve your purposes for a fulfilling, well-remunerated and worthy career of your choice. So many have gone before you, vainly hoping that they'll get spotted in the crowd. Plucked from the sea of mediocrity, dusted down and propelled to stardom. The keys to the boardroom are not always held by those people who see your best work. And unless they're compelled or inspired to talk about you, you'll remain in the pool of talent with everyone else.

Somewhere down the line you're going to have to get out there and sell your wares. You're going to need agents, sponsors, advocates and word of mouth allies. You're going to need connections and introductions. You're going to need a platform or shop window for your opinions and ideas. You're going to need a presence and a profile. You need a reputation.

Of course, marketing yourself brilliantly, interviewing effortlessly and being your own number-one fan is redundant if you're actually no good ...

2. The trap of being ordinary or even just good

They say you can't polish a turd. It's no good being everywhere and being lousy. Advertising legend David Ogilvy claimed: '*Great marketing only makes a bad product fail faster.*' You can market the crap out of anything, but if it's a lousy product, it's only going to get rejected by the marketplace.

Actually, forget being lousy. You can't even afford to be good. Everyone is good. Good gets you in the game. Great gets you on the podium. *Being good used to be a differentiator. Now it's just a qualifier.* It used to set you apart. Now it just gets you a ticket to the concert.

So the message is to ~~be brilliant in some way~~. Seth Godin says: *'You're either remarkable or invisible.'* If you're better, different, remarkable or great, you've got a chance to trade up. You've got an opportunity to win the game. You've got the career capital and the means to shape your career in the way YOU want it to go. And that's priceless.

The power of the plan and the action

The hustling part of the deal is important. You can build the most incredible car in the world, but it still needs driving. So what exactly does hustle mean? The mainstream dictionaries offer up the following:

- energetic action
- determination
- hard work
- rapid movement
- noise and activity
- to push or nudge things forward
- to make people or situations move quickly
- to grasp opportunities.

I like the more urban definitions, though let's leave the illegal stuff out of our game plan:

'Anythin you need to do to make money ... be it sellin cars, drugs, ya body. If you makin money, you hustlin. I been workin two jobs, tryna stay on my hustle and make this money, na mean?'

~~Hustling is action on steroid~~s. The hustle is the dynamite, the impetus and the fuel that makes the plan happen. You need hustle to get up, get out and get ahead. Without it, doors will close in front of you. Your rivals will get ahead of you. Opportunities will appear brightly before you and then fade away. Take a step. Make a move. Get hustling!

The plan is the due diligence. The roadmap. The playbook. The blueprint. With hustle and no plan, you're just ignorance on fire.

There's huge power in the plan. Some heavy lifting and planning up front will chart your course. Strategy is the art of thinking. It's how you'll bring about your end goal. It works in war, politics, sports and business. It works in the Career Game too.

You need a proper strategy to create a credible and desirable reputation, and the action plan to lift it into the minds of your target audience. That way, when they need what you do, they think of you first, above and beyond all of their other choices. Together with your hustle, your game plan turns you into a Career Pro. It helps you play to win.

Playing to win the career game

So, we've looked at who you're up against. The Fatalist, the Planner and the Hustler. Hopefully none of them are you, which makes you a Career Pro. You're purposeful and strategic, yet opportunistic and random. You want to be the number-one choice for what you do. You've got big career plans and you want in. You're ready to play, and you're ready to do the practise it takes to play well.

'If I don't practise like I know I should, I won't play like I know I can.'
– Ivan Lendl

You know the common mistakes and you're determined not to make them. You don't want to leave your career to chance. Hoping you'll get that promotion only gets you so far. Even being told you'll get it and sitting back waiting for the call is too reactive.

Only so many people get the best jobs. Only so many make partner or reach the boardroom. Only so many get the opportunity to do work they love and live out a fulfilled career. That's why most business structures are pyramids. Lots at the bottom, few at the top.

Ask your friends and colleagues how many of them really 'get to do their job' rather than 'have to do their job'. Not many. But you can by being a Career Pro. Only the Career Pro has the right blend of proactivity and strategy, hustle and planning to create the best possible career trading positions.

If the object of the game is to win, then you've simply got to become so good they can't ignore you.

So good they can't ignore you

Cal Newport is a professor of computer science at Georgetown and author of the brilliant book *So Good They Can't Ignore – Why Skills Trump Passion in the Quest for Work You Love*. In it, he tells the story of comedian Steve Martin being interviewed on the Charlie Rose show in 2007 about his comedy career. Rose asked him for his advice to aspiring performers. His response was eloquent:

> *'Nobody ever takes note of [my advice], because it's not the answer they wanted to hear. What they want to hear is "Here's how you get an agent, here's how you write a script," but I always say, "Be so good they can't ignore you."'*

Newport elegantly calls this career capital – your currency to trade for the work, the opportunities and the stuff you love. It's your leverage. Without it, you'll never be in a position to trade up.

Seth Godin thinks along similar lines in *LinchPin: Are You Indispensable?* He states:

'The only way to get what you're worth is to stand out, to exert emotional labor, to be seen as indispensable, and to produce interactions that organizations and people care deeply about.'

This book is your manual for not just acquiring that career capital, but marketing yourself in such a way that people know you're in the game. That's where your good name, your profile and your personal reputation come in. If you don't market yourself properly, you'll be brilliant but anonymous. Can you afford that?

A game worth playing

Is it worth fighting for a job you really enjoy? Or is it just a fact of life that work is work and 'you just have to get on with it'? After all, you're lucky to have a job at all, right?

The truth is that work is not universally popular. Reports into job satisfaction and engagement tell us that most people are unhappy at work. Forbes cited a Gallup poll from 2013 of 25 million employees in 189 different countries with the news that unhappy employees outnumber happy ones by two to one worldwide. Google 'job satisfaction surveys' and you'll find that if you're less than satisfied with your current job or future career path, you're not alone.

Men tend to be slightly happier than women. Drudgery (boredom) and bad bosses are troublesome for many, but the most common worry is layoffs and job security. Insecurity runs deep. Almost nobody is safe. Private sector or public, good economy or bad, big company or small. You're in the soup with the rest of us, and it's your responsibility to ensure you can withstand the uncertainty of a turbulent employment landscape.

If these findings resonate with you, then the Career Game might be one worth playing. If your brilliance, your reputation and your career capital can be traded, you can engineer a career that gives you what makes employees happy in their jobs. Things like impactful and meaningful work, control and autonomy, creativity and interest, choice, decent compensation and benefits, respectful treatment and job security. These are what will make you connected and committed to your work and engaged with your career. Now isn't that worth buying a ticket to the game?

The ultimate rewards

We are all wired up differently and all motivated by different things. What causes you to do certain things may not have an effect on me. When you play and win the Career Game, you get to decide what you want in return for your valuable contribution and great reputation. In addition to work that you love and that inspires you. The following benefits are also on offer – popularity, prosperity and pleasure.

If you tend to be more driven by popularity (the public recognition and validation of others) then the following benefits accrue from a good reputation and doing a great job:

- love and adulation
- status and kudos
- admiration and acknowledgement
- fame and reverence
- approval and acceptance.

If you're more prosperity focused (motivated by money and material things), then these benefits are usually made available to those people with a successful career and a strong name:

- new business, sales, deals and clients
- income and wealth
- security and peace of mind
- possessions, trinkets and clothes

- holidays or vacations
- bonuses, rewards and commissions
- perks and privileges.

Finally, if your key drivers tend to be more pleasure-oriented (hedonistic and self-indulgent), then rest assured that an investment in your career and your reputation will likely result in more of these in your life:

- contentment and satisfaction
- excitement and passion
- enjoyment and happiness
- purpose and fulfilment
- time and space
- direction and purpose
- interesting projects, ventures and opportunities
- career options and job choice.

No guarantees

You know you've got to play. You're competing for a limited number of the best jobs and most fulfilling careers. You're fighting for choice, control and meaning in your work. But you could play right and still lose. There are no guarantees.

Here's a quick disclaimer on the Career Game. Just because you're in it, and even if you win it, nothing is guaranteed. So much is out of your control. This playbook inoculates you against the worst and sets you up for the best. Shit happens, right?

You can have a rewarding and varied career. But it might not happen for you. There are too many unknowns. What can be said is this. Protect yourself with a decent store of career capital, a powerful reputation and a formidable network. Put yourself in a strong trading position to win the Career Game.

When you become an authority in your field, surround yourself with powerful, useful people; you've got a lottery ticket. You've got a few lottery tickets! It's less likely you'll be laid off. It's more likely you'll find the right job quickly if you do. So buy a ticket and let's play the game!

Summary: Setting the scene – the career game

You're in a game, whether you like it or not. The stakes are your life and your career. There are rules to be followed and exploited to give you the best possible career choices. You can open doors and create choice if you can trade your brilliance and your great name for the career choice and fulfilment you desire. Good leaders have followers and advocates before they are promoted. You can do the same because this is all coachable.

Your ultimate career aim is work you love on your terms. Life on your terms sounds sweet. What might that look like? It comes down to one word. CHOICE. The ability to choose where and how you make your way is the single biggest driver in our lives. To have that kind of choice, you have to compete and win in this Career Game.

You know now that this is a trading game where you swap valuable career capital for the opportunity to do the kind of work that excites you, rewards you and fulfils you. You trade your contribution for choice. Cal Newport says that rare and valuable career characteristics, like creativity, impact, control, reward and choice, require rare and valuable traits that you can trade in return.

You now recognize the four types of career builder you might be. You've seen the mistakes that get made in the Career Game. To win any game, or even just to do well, it's vital to know the rules of the game. What works and what doesn't. What's allowed and what isn't.

You need to be that proactive, strategic Career Pro – the one with the great reputation, great connections and irresistible presence that people pay top dollar for. Only career capital and a powerful reputation will land you the career YOU choose, not somebody else.

As a Career Pro, you have two great weapons to make it happen for you. A strategy or game plan. And the hustle to execute. With these you can focus your time and effort on what will increase your chances of winning. Once you're in the game, you'll see the power of getting connected and making a telling contribution to the world. Building-blocks and commodities you'll trade up for more career options.

Let's get to work!

Chapter 3

Your Reputation Game Plan

'There is only one thing in the world worse than being talked about, and that is not being talked about.'

– Oscar Wilde

The ultimate aim of the career game

In this chapter, you'll start out building your career enhancing reputation by seeing where you are right now. You've seen what a reputation is and what it can do for you. You've studied the rules and you're committed to the cause. You're excited about the prospect of playing the Career Game. You're keen to get started.

Your ultimate aim and primary objective: *work you love on your terms*. Here's a list of what this could look like for you. It's not exclusive. You can add anything else to the list that means more choice, creativity, impact, control and reward.

For now, try any of these for size and see if they get you excited about building an outstanding reputation and a big heap of career capital. Because that's the only way you're going to get:

- Your place in the boardroom.
- A partner or director role (say with a salary, share or equity option).
- Your next promotion.
- A particular role in the company (why not the CEO?).
- The invitation to work for a competitor.
- A leadership or management role.
- Your place on a particular talent or leadership development programme.

- More power in your current role (more influence, respect or honour).
- The power to change your current working situation to your advantage, say for work–life balance, health, travel or fulfilment reasons).
- An opportunity to do more meaningful work that you're passionate about.
- The approval to start your own project or run your own team.
- The platform, credibility and career capital to go off and do your own entrepreneurial thing.
- The financial independence to quit or retire.
- The blessing to take a sabbatical.
- More money, a decent pay rise or a bigger and better bonus structure.
- Better working conditions.
- A more comprehensive work package of perks and benefits.
- The chance to work with a particular person or team or on a project.
- The flexibility and backing to move to a different part of the organization.
- Security and protection from layoff in your current position (which you absolutely love).

Do all of these sound good? You know the rules of the Career Game. That these jobs and opportunities don't come around too often. They're not open to everyone. Anything better and different constitutes an exceptional opportunity. To be worthy, you've got to offer something exceptional in return.

The 12 things that make you valuable

To be exceptional, you need career capital. You've got to make your star shine so bright that the people that count notice it. You're going to build a number-one, 'go-to', obvious choice, stand-out, formidable reputation that makes giving you what you want a no-brainer. You get that generating career capital brings you career choices. The power to trade for work you love on your terms.

Perhaps you're wondering whether your reputation is the same thing as career capital. The answer is that reputation is a component of career capital. It's all linked. You could argue that your reputation is another word for career capital. But there are 12 things that make you valuable and generate that career capital for you. Reputation is one of them. Here's the whole list:

1. **Reputation** – a powerful name that invokes trust, credibility and authority.
2. **Connections** – your reach, following and contacts – relationship capital.
3. **Executive presence** – your ability to gain high-level engagement.
4. **Influence** – the ability to make people act, think or believe.
5. **Skills** – the stuff you do better than almost everyone else.
6. **Knowledge** – the stuff you know more about than most others.
7. **Creativity** – your ability to generate great ideas, plans and projects.
8. **Usefulness** - to help, advise and solve problems.
9. **Likeability** – being easy and fun to be around.
10. **Hustle** – your attitude to take risks and act aggressively.
11. **Productivity** – the ability work smart and get things quickly.
12. **Achievement** – a track record of good results.
13. **Attitude** – your desire, enthusiasm and approach to life and work.

This list is not exclusive but it is comprehensive. This inventory of career capital has to be earned, practised and traded for. You can't just claim it by genetics or birthright. We are all born with talents, but not everyone turns those gifts into strengths and competitive advantages.

You'll be focusing on one of these but you can easily see that our framework encompasses many of the others. It's compound interest.

Nail any one of these and it will positively affect your capacity in multiple others. For instance, increase your relationship capital and that will have a profound impact on your productivity, your reputation, your usefulness and your influence.

So you're ready to build. You'll spend a short time on where you are now and where you want to be. But then it's about bridging that gap. The good stuff. *How do you get better? How do you really become well-known?* So here's the game plan. For this chapter, you're going to do a little bit of work on your foundation, or your primary core.

What's your current reputation?

Your foundation for a stand-out reputation starts on the inside. These are your raw materials or building blocks. There are four:

1. **Your character**. Your core values and life principles.
2. **Your personality**. Your unique attributes.
3. **Your strengths**. The stuff you're really good at.
4. **Your passions**. The stuff you really enjoy doing.

If your reputation is congruent and authentic, then it should be an extension of your core. What's on the inside will be reflected on the outside. Get this right and you'll be playing to your strengths. Don't worry – this won't involve too much introspection!

So let's take a closer look at these four core components: character, personality, strengths and passions.

Core component 1: Your character

What's the difference between character and personality? Your personality is those distinctive personal qualities and attributes you were born with.

This describes how creative, academic or practical you are. It describes whether you are gentle or aggressive, introvert or extrovert, loud or quiet, driven or laid-back, optimistic or pessimistic, risk-taking or cautious, selfless or selfish. These attributes are not easy to change. They are inborn. They are an indispensable part of you.

Your character is those values and beliefs you cling to and hold dear. Examples are integrity, honesty and compassion. You can develop these over time and they are shaped as much by circumstances as genetics.

Both of these will influence your behaviour, which is the outward expression of your character and personality. When you wrap them altogether, they make up a very unique you!

It's pretty easy to identify your core values. You're saying what's important to you and checking you're living that out. A core value is something you really believe in; something that is truly important to you. It defines your character. They are usually based on moral or ethical principles. What's important to you. They are the rocks in your life. There is little room for deviation or change, whatever the circumstances.

Here are the most common 64 core personal values. Which ones hold true for you? Which are the most important to you? Around 4–6 is ideal. Any more than that becomes difficult to monitor and sustain. Some seem similar, like truth and honesty, or joy and happiness. However, specific words may suit you, your character and your aspirations.

Identifying your core values helps you see on a deep level what truly matters to you and motivates you. It tells you what you'll hold on to when the seas get a little rough. Remember: your character is reflected through your actions, thoughts and words to the outside world, and this is what makes or breaks your reputation.

Influence	Recognition	Kindness	Fame
Family	Wealth	Happiness	Effort
Truth	Compassion	Status	Attitude
Innovation	Wisdom	Success	Strength
Integrity	Creativity	Authenticity	Love
Security	Honour	Accountability	Loyalty
Fun	Flexibility	Peace	Persistence
Honesty	Learning	Commitment	Spirituality
Respect	Faith	Fairness	Collaboration
Adventure	Cooperation	Dependability	Contribution
Support	Courage	Freedom	Justice
Friendship	Trust	Connectedness	Resourcefulness
Understanding	Service	Beauty	Charity
Generosity	Dedication	Power	Excellence

Core component 2. Your personality

Personality traits are your distinguishing qualities. They make you think or act in certain ways. They seldom vary. Once you have them, you have them, although they can evolve. For instance, studies show that women tend to become more dominant, independent and self-confident over time.

In 1936, two researchers (Allport and Odbert) found 17,953 personality traits describing the ways you are psychologically different from others (e.g. shy, trustworthy, laconic, phlegmatic, kind, conscientious, anxious). Another researcher, Cattell, narrowed this listing down to 16 personality factors:

1. Reserved vs. Warm
2. Concrete Reasoning vs. Abstract Reasoning
3. Reactive vs. Emotionally Stable
4. Deferential vs. Dominant
5. Serious vs. Lively
6. Expedient vs. Rule-Conscious

7. Shy vs. Socially Bold
8. Utilitarian vs. Sensitive
9. Trusting vs. Vigilant
10. Practical vs. Imaginative
11. Forthright vs. Private
12. Self-Assured vs. Apprehensive
13. Traditional vs. Open-To-Change
14. Group-Oriented vs. Self-Reliant
15. Tolerates Disorder vs. Perfectionist
16. Relaxed vs. Tense

Each dynamic is a continuum with many shades between the extremes. This explains why you are unique. You have that distinctive set of values and characteristics which make you you!

How does this affect your reputation? Well, your reputation is simply people's opinion of you. Once people make up their minds, it's very difficult to change them. This is good for you if you create a strong initial impression. But may make problems for you down the line if that impression is a weak or negative one.

Research shows that you like people who are similar to you in their opinions, personality traits, background or lifestyle. Lesson – to be liked and rated, exhibit the qualities those people find attractive and appealing.

If you have negative traits that upset people, put them off you, or make you difficult to deal with, you will find it difficult to create a positive reputation. If you have great personality traits, play on them.

Core component 3: Your strengths

What are you really good at? You'll probably make your most valuable contribution and your biggest impact in an area of strength. The fact is, you're irreplaceable. There's nobody quite like you. If you believe it, God did a great job of making you 100% unique.

There are things you're so amazing at, it would just blow me away. Likewise, you might be amazed at how good this book is and how it's something you could never write. Maybe. Point is, we're made differently, brought up differently and trained differently. We have different strengths and abilities. Weaknesses and flaws.

How do you become stand-out brilliant and do lots of stuff you love? Well, conventional wisdom says shore up your weaknesses. Work on your flaws. Bring yourself up to standard. That way you can be that all-round good employee. The problem is that spending time fixing your shortcomings doesn't allow you to do what you do best every day. What if you left the weaknesses to themselves and focused on your strengths? This approach has some merit.

A strength is something you can do incredibly well, easily and consistently. It's near perfect performance on a consistent basis in a particular area. It's a combination of your talents (natural gifts and abilities) and how you've invested in those talents with training, education and practice.

Your strengths are honed talents. And they make a powerful and significant contribution to your reputation. A few questions to help you decide what your strengths could be[1]:

- What are you really good at?
- What could you be the best at?
- What are you most proud of in your working life?
- What stands out most in your skill set?

---

[1] Also check out the Strengths Manifesto found in the Reputation Vault. It covers exactly what strengths are, how to identify them and how to exploit them for reputational advantage. The book *Strengthsfinder 2.0* by Tom Rath also features an online test to reveal your top five strengths.

- What do you know more about than most?
- What have you achieved that is worth boasting about?

Core component 4. Your passions

You may be familiar with the career book *What Colour Is Your Parachute?* by Richard Nelson Bolles. It's still in print. This and almost every other career book and career expert have extolled a Passion Hypothesis.

The Passion Hypothesis says you have pre-existing passions that you must match to a job if you want to be happy in work. This will probably frustrate you because what you're passionate about is often not what you can create a meaningful career out of.

It turns out that trying to follow your passions into work is really bad advice, according to Cal Newport in *So Good They Can't Ignore You*. For example, legendary Apple founder Steve Jobs was a hippy wandering around an American college campus back in the day. He showed no real passion or talent for computers. If he'd followed his passion, he'd probably have ended up as a Buddhist monk or spiritualist teacher. Newport cites plenty more similar examples.

The danger of chasing your passion is that as soon as you begin feeling dissatisfied about your work, you start dreaming about some other magic job which will cater more for your passions. The passion mindset selfishly demands the world give you the perfect job.

A better approach is to create career capital, work on yourself and your skills and create the job of your dreams with all the choice, control, autonomy and freedom you can. If you find a job that plays right to your passions, you've done well. For the other 99.9% of people, working right trumps finding the right work.

This is not to discount your passions. If you want to factor them into your quest for career capital, here are a few guiding questions:

- What do you love doing?
- What gets you excited?
- What makes you want to go into work?
- What makes you stay late?
- What aspects of your job give you most joy?
- What gives you meaning?
- What most matches your core values?
- What kind of work gives you the most satisfaction?
- What was the most interesting project you've worked on recently?

To conclude, your passions are important, but don't lean too heavily on them to find great work you love. Think about what you can offer the world rather than what the world can offer you. Then you'll put your passions in the right perspective.

So that's the four core components of your reputation – character, personality, strengths and passions. Ground your reputation building in those and you'll create something compelling, authentic and powerful.

Perhaps you're still pining for the old approach to crafting your killer reputation. Maybe you yearn for a little navel-gazing and contemplation just to check you've covered all the bases. Let's see what we can do for you.

Eight ways to define your current reputation

A good reputation sets you apart. So it might be useful to know exactly what your reputation is if you're going to enhance or change it. For that reason, I'd like to appease your desire to go 'old school' and help you get a handle on your current reputation.

Your current reputation is something you've purposefully and diligently crafted and marketed to the whole world. Or it's something that evolved by accident because you allowed people to make up their own minds about you. I accept it's useful to know what that is.

So here are eight clever tools and strategies to find your start point. As a beginning for your global domination plan, they'll tell you what you're playing with. It's the 'where are you now?' moment. They'll help you assess what raw materials you've got to play with and how you can shape them into the career capital you're looking for. If nothing else, they're fun!

Why do you need eight? You don't. But you've got a choice. One might be perfect for you. I just don't know which one. But hopefully you will when you see it.

1. What's in your red box?

What's in Your Red Box?

COPY

CLAIM

- YOU!
- Relationships
- Ideas
- Reputation
- Knowledge
- Experience
- Expertise
- Connections
- Contribution
- Content

Not so long back I delivered a TEDx talk in the UK called the Personal Brand of You: What's in Your Red Box? The essence of the presentation was that 90% of what you do is done by your competitors, however you define them.

This is represented by the big grey box. In order to stand out, you must create or leverage the stuff your competition cannot easily copy or claim. Stuff that's in your red box. You don't need to be radically different. Just different enough that you're perceived to be different.

That means coming up with the most unique stuff you can. When I do this exercise with companies and ask them how or where they are different, they talk about their great service, their rich history their customer centric values, their big vision or their talented people. They don't realize that their rivals are claiming the same unique points of differentiation.

Better is their intellectual property, their brand and their proprietary products or services. Their charity links or green credentials. Even any unique ways they serve their customers.

For personal brands like you, it's slightly different. You've got to leverage your personal aspects. As you learned earlier, these are your values, your character, your strengths (ideas, skills, knowledge, connections, contribution), your personal brand and ultimately your reputation. Nobody can copy or claim this stuff. It's uniquely yours.

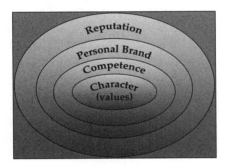

Here's your red box up close. Consider this as we try to distil what you will create to establish your reputation and authority status.

2. The reality gap exercise

This looks at the gap between how you rate yourself and how you think others rate you. Rank each side with a score from 1 to 10 based on how you rate yourself in these areas, and how you think others rate you. It's a fun task but also gives you valuable insight into whether you think more of yourself than others do.

Your Reputation			Your Self-Esteem	
What others think of you			What you think of yourself	
How others see you			How you see yourself	
External			Internal	
1 ←			→ 10 High	
		The way you talk		
		The way you walk		
		The way you sing		
		The way you look naked		
		The way you dance		
		The way you network		
		The way you treat your clients and customers		
		The way you dress		
		How smart you are		
		How healthy you are		
		How organized you are		
		How punctual you are		
		How much fun you are		
		How reliable you are		
		How positive and optimistic you are		
		How negative and pessimistic you are		
		How forgiving you are		
		How patient you are		
		How good you are at your job		
		How good you are at your hobby/sport		
		How well you write		
		How well you create ideas		
		How well you present		
		How well you relate to authority		
		How well you relate to your colleagues		
		How well you relate to subordinates		
		How you handle challenge and adversity		
		How persistent you are		
		TOTALS		

3. The SWOT analysis

You'll be very familiar with this, but may not have used it before in laying the foundations for your personal reputation. SWOT stands for Strengths, Weaknesses, Opportunities and Threats. This builds on the positives and looks at ways of converting your weaknesses and threats into strengths and opportunities. Here is the format. I've added some questions to help you articulate answers in each area.

STRENGTHS	WEAKNESSES
What do others see as your strengths?	Where do you have fewer resources than others?
What unique resources can you draw on?	What flaws might trip you up in the future?
What do you do better than most other people?	What could you possibly improve?
What advantages do you have over your rivals?	What are others likely to see as your weaknesses?
OPPORTUNITIES	THREATS
What good opportunities are open to you?	What threats could be harming you?
What trends could you take advantage of?	What is your competition doing particularly well?
How could you turn strengths into opportunities?	What threats might your weaknesses expose you to?

If you don't do introspection, or you have no clue what these answers are, you've got two options. First, identify some good people who can help tease these answers out of you. Second, ask some of your stakeholders exactly what they think about you.

4. Peer appraisal

If you want to know what other people think of you, there's a simple way to find out. ASK! The trick is to ask courageously and ask the right people – your stakeholders. Of course, if you're going to solicit the opinions of people who you care about (and presumably who care about you) then you've got to be open to straight talk. You must be open to whatever your friends, peers, clients, customers, associates, superiors, mentors and employees say and think about you. Warts and all.

There are a couple of ways to do this. First is with a quick survey. Identify 6–10 people (work and personal) who know you well enough to comment and put together a few questions you'd like answered about yourself. If you go to the Reputation Vault, we've done you a **Peer Appraisal Manifesto.** It gives you a great one-page survey you can use. You also get some great scripts to help you position it.

A second, more informal way is to engineer a few corridor or coffee moments to 'pop a question'. You simply tell a trusted friend that you're doing some personal development work and ask them to describe you in a 3–5 words. Or ask what other people say when they talk about you. You'll find some great scripts and ideas on how to do this in the **Peer Appraisal Manifesto**.

Obviously you'll start to see the same words and phrases coming up. These patterns will reveal your reputation – what people think, do, feel and say when they come across you and your name. If you're courageous with this, ask them to throw one negative one in there. Say you're looking for blind spots, potential weaknesses and stuff you can work on. Fortune favours the brave.

5. UVP analysis

Your Unique Value Selling Proposition (UVP) is similar to a USP (Unique Selling Proposition) but is more than just a description. It's your competitive advantage in the Career Game. It's your distinctive career market position. It's why people come to you, buy you and even sell you. It's what you can offer that your competitors can't. It's the stuff you wrap your personal marketing and thought leadership around.

Without any differentiators, you're a mere commodity in a race to the bottom. You'll lose out to people who are just the same or just as good. Sometimes even not as good, but definitely cheaper.

Your UVP begins to explain the difference you would like to make by articulating why you're different to your competition and why people should choose you over them. For instance, why should people hire or promote or work with YOU, as opposed to someone else who offers the same thing you do? What value, what results, what solutions and what relief can you bring to the company, your boss, your team, your department that they cannot easily get anywhere else?

It's not easy to articulate a UVP. If you have one that's working for you, others will want to copy it, just like if it was a product or service, not an individual. Done right, it says 'choose me, for this specific reason'.

A UVP should also be something your competition struggles to offer, hence the word unique. It should also be of value to your stakeholders. No good having a USP of wearing only yellow socks or being brilliant at jigsaws if nobody cares.

To figure out your potential UVP, ask what your employers, customers, clients and stakeholders really value. Examples include experience, specialist knowledge, sales skills, likeability, ease of working with, creativity, reliability, integrity, profile, connections, ability to work fast or hit deadlines, focus, productivity, languages and delivery.

Now rank yourself and up to three of your colleagues or competitors by those same criteria out of 10. If you've got hard data to back up your scores, great. If not, estimate from the stakeholder's perspective. Now see where you rank well and where you don't. How do you stack up head to head?

Once you've got a UVP, make it known. Communicate it, defend it and hone it. Keep working on your craft because it makes you hard to keep up with. Build it up and even morph it into something new and improved. Clear water between you and them, right?

6. Core competences exercise

Outsourcing is focusing your efforts on stuff you do well and offloading as much as you can of everything else. It is successful on a corporate level and is a useful personal marketing concept. When you align your core competencies with your company's, you're adding value. You're also less likely to be 'superfluous to requirements'.

Core competencies came to prominence in a flagship 1990 paper 'The Core Competence of the Corporation,' by C.K. Prahalad and Gary Hamel. They define core competences as the things a company does uniquely well, and that no one else can copy quickly enough to affect competition. They give examples of dinosaur companies who became extinct because they didn't see and exploit their strengths. They also provide three tests to check whether a competence is truly unique:

1. **Relevance**. Does it make you more attractive and 'choosable'? If it doesn't strengthen your career position, make you more competitive and add to your influence, then it's not a core competence.
2. **Difficulty of imitation**. Is it hard to duplicate or replicate? Any 'barrier to entry' discourages your competition from trying to catch you up or occupy your space.
3. **Breadth of application**. Does it create opportunities? If you can leverage it to open up new markets, bring in new business and create good growth, you've got something.

To illustrate, you might have strong sales skills in your arsenal. Relevance? Yes – the ability to sell will always be in demand. Difficult to imitate? Yes, as not everyone is comfortable selling. Breadth of application? Yes, as sales drive growth. Overall score: 3 out of 3. Promising. Try this with things like industry knowledge or language expertise and see how you come out.

Like USPs, you're looking for uniqueness with your core competences. That means any 'me too' comparisons that make you indistinguishable from your rivals. Once you've got something, you can wrap a reputation around it by building it up and out. In doing so, you move away from your weak areas.

7. Psychometric tests

Obvious really. If you want to figure out what you're good at and what you're suited to, do a test. There are many types. Some focus on specific skills. Others are personality based. Most companies and recruiters use them. They can be useful in finding out what you're really like and what you're really good at. An overview of the most common types:

- **Aptitude**. Measure ability, intelligence or knowledge level in a certain field.
- **Verbal reasoning**. Measures understanding. Sometimes spelling, grammar and syntax.
- **Numerical reasoning**. Measures mathematical capability.
- **Abstract reasoning**. Measures problem solving and analytical thinking.
- **Personality**. Measures how you work in certain situations.
- **Motivation**. Measures what drives you and inspires you.
- **Accuracy**. Measures your checking and observational ability.
- **Knowledge**. Measures your proficiency in a certain field or area, e.g. engineering or IT.

You name it, there's a test for it – IQ, EQ, sales aptitude, management capability, leadership qualities, logic, relationship and communication skills, languages, stress, organizational skills, creativity, writing. Whatever you want to know about yourself, you can figure it out with some kind of test.

8. The ultimate test – self-assessment

It's likely that nobody knows you better than you. If you've got any degree of self-awareness, then you probably know what you're good at and what you're not. Go with your instinct.

It's all there. It's in your LinkedIn profile or your Twitter bio. Maybe in previous employment evaluations or a feedback report. Come on, you're not stupid. You're not ignorant. You know where you're good and where you're weak. What you like and what you don't. Here are four useful areas to begin self-assessing your reputation:

1. **Your word of mouth**. When your name is mentioned in your absence, what are people thinking and saying?
2. **Your track record**. How have your failures and successes defined you?
3. **Your actions**. What are you doing or not doing that is enhancing or destroying your personal brand?
4. **Your network**. Who are you associating with? What does your network say about you?

These are not easy to answer without a certain degree of thought and introspection. Some of the other tools and strategies may help. You actually don't need to pinpoint a starting point nor an accurate final destination. A general sense of where you are and a loose sense of heading in the right direction will do. Like a climber heading up a wall or a driver in heavy fog. Go a little further and the next handhold or piece of tarmac becomes visible. Sounds trite but trust your gut. Follow your heart. Back yourself.

What to do if you have no reputation

Perhaps you've asked a few people what they think of you and just got blank stares. Tumbleweed. Are you sure you're totally anonymous? People must think something of you. They're probably just getting a weak signal. You're a well-kept secret, right?

This is actually quite common. Your reputation does nothing for you because it's too feeble and light. It usually happens when:

- You've got no 'stand-out' speciality area.

- You're new in a role and have not had the chance to establish yourself.
- Your client portfolio is too wide-ranging to pick out any definable group.
- You're young and relatively inexperienced.
- You've got too many areas of speciality and you're struggling to 'pick a lane'.

In these scenarios, the career marketplace is telling you something. You're not ready. This can be a great place to be. Blank canvas. A clear shot at goal. You're stood at the buffet with a big empty plate. Your game plan should be to try everything. Talk to everyone. Be everywhere. Taste and see. Take some risks. Try some things.

Get into the Reputation Toolboxes in Part Two. Get networking, get creating and get online. Raise your profile and work on your skills. Embrace serendipity. Take some risks. When your time comes, you'll be ready.

Summary: Your reputation game plan

So, if it's important to you, you've just figured out where you are. You've taken stock of your current reputation. You now know where you're starting from and what raw materials you're playing with. You've maybe even focused on the differences between you and your competitors.

You're looking ahead to what you want to be known for and by whom. Your final destination. Your ideal job, career or reputation. It need not be laid out in minute detail. But some kind of roadmap and loose destination might be of benefit. Your vision of the future. Some kind of blueprint design or career end-goal. With a good sense of what you want, you can start developing the career capital and reputation to take you there.

What if you don't know where you're going? You actually may not have an end-goal for your career. Just some 'gut feeling' that you want the best possible career you can get. That's okay. Maybe you've skipped the above self-contemplation because you already know you're pretty good and you just want to keep getting better; I get that. You just want to get on with it.

You want more control and choice in your career. If you don't know exactly what that looks like, at least you know it means becoming more valuable and exceptional. Various things such as your reputation, your skills, your attitude, your likeability, your knowledge and your influence make you valuable. This constitutes career capital that you can trade for control, choice and meaning in your career.

Building on your core of character, personality, strengths and passions, you're ready to move. You've got four Reputation Toolboxes coming up. These are not done one step after another. You can do them all at the same time.

In Part Two of the book, you'll unpack the four Reputation Toolboxes. These are what will deliver you the Holy Grail of work you love on your terms. These are your keys to unlock a formidable, extraordinary reputation that will make it easy for others to promote you and protect you. Before that, it's essential you nail two critical areas of reputation management. Your network (for visibility, profile, advocacy and opportunities) and your authority (for expert status, power positioning and a stand-out reputation. Here are the blueprints ...

Chapter 4

The Networking Blueprint

'Your network is who you know. Your reputation is who knows you. When you grow the first, you grow the second.'

– Rob Brown

The power of your network in reputation building

Your network will open doors for you. It will make you a better leader and a better team player. It amplifies your voice and magnifies your contribution to the cause. Yet most people struggle with building a network.

Networking is simply talking and listening. Building and leveraging relationships. It's not a dark art or mysterious science. The problem is that it's just not taught or trained well. It's not on the curriculum. It's not a professional qualification or academic accreditation. It's rarely offered in an 'on the job' training programme.

As a result, too many high-quality technically-gifted and academically-loaded people struggle with it. Yet it's vital for you in your quest for career capital and reputational influence. Instinctively you know that.

From your personal perspective, your network is a valuable piece of the career capital jigsaw. The people you associate with and can call upon for help say much about you as a person.

As you move up the ladder, you'll be aware of critical transition points. Your peer group changes. Your perspective on what's important changes. What you spend your time on changes. Who you need alongside you changes.

The people you currently associate with can enhance or undermine your reputation. You may have heard the old saying 'show me your friends and I will predict your future'. You tend to become like the people you spend the most time with.

You naturally aspire to become those people you look up to and into. That's why celebrities are not the best role models. You don't have to go far to find one with drug problems, relationship issues and psychological flaws. There are enough mere mortals to associate with who will do wonders for your reputation.

So, here's the headline. Your network is who you know. Your reputation is who knows you. Your network is always smaller than your reputation. There will always be more people out there who know you or of you that you've never even met. That's because people will talk about you to those you don't know. And your words, your voice, your brand, your art, your stuff will be out there on show to the world in front of people you'll never meet. This is why they say 'your reputation goes before you'.

Your reputation will always exceed your network. And the bigger and better you can grow your network, the bigger and better you can grow your reputation. In other words, work hard and smart to build your connections, for your network feeds your reputation.

If you associate with people who match your own values, dreams and aspirations, then you'll find the right level of empathy and support when you need it. If you foster relationships with people who can fill in the gaps of your weaknesses and complement your strengths, you'll soon become the finished article with tons of career capital. After all, maybe you can't do it, but you know who can, right?

As a strategic networker and career builder, it's your job to source and nurture these relationships. Hopefully before you need them. And then use them in the right way to excel your performance and achieve your career objectives. Once you know what you want, you're closer to defining who you want.

This is why you need to build and leverage a formidable, diverse network of all kinds of people. Not just for the assistance they'll give you in kicking on. But for the kudos of simply being associated with them.

When it comes to developing career capital and getting on the radars of all the right people, your network feeds your reputation. You need a Networking Blueprint, which starts with calibrating your current network. Who do you know right now?

Calibrating your network

The right people and the right connections won't always come to you. Usually you've got to go to them. This is what creates your network. Your network is one of the two biggest engines to build your reputation (the other is your authority or expert status). So how do you go about building one?

The first step in building and leveraging a formidable network is to look at your start point. What have you got? What do you need? Where are the gaps? There are all kinds of people you need on your team bus. What kind of shape is your networking in right now?

They say the best time to plant a tree is 20 years ago. The worst time is now. A network is similar. It's better if you started a long time ago, because it would be awesome now. But you've got to start somewhere. In the Reputation Building Toolboxes there are tons of ways to build your network. For now, be concerned with who you need around you to aid you in your career quest.

If you're starting out, it will be more social than professional. Up to the age of 30 is party time. Social media mayhem. You're all over Facebook or Twitter or Instagram sharing your interesting life. Then it starts to get serious.

Who are you playing with currently? Take a long hard look at your email list, your LinkedIn connections, your social media followers and your phone contacts. You'll see if you've got the right people on your team bus. Remember: the network you have right now has got you where you are. It's probably not adequate to get you where you need to be.

You'll need to build up and out. To fill those gaps. To get the right people around you. To create an inner circle of confidantes and advisors. And of course an outer circle of followers, friends and fans. Then you fill in the gaps. Round it out. Take it up a few levels. There are three main approaches to view and build your network. Let's find out more ...

The three approaches to build your network

Putting together a network of individuals that works for you takes a bit of doing. A network is a collection of individuals who know you or at least know *of* you. The ideal network is deep, diverse and varied. It generates career capital for you and elevates your reputation by association. It cuts across countries, cultures and boundaries. It's a blend of personal, social and professional. It's levels above you, below you and to your left and right.

It comprises certain kinds of people you can trust. It gives you loyalty, ability and integrity. It covers gaps and blind-spots. It provides expertise and knowledge. It gives you connections and influence. It offers critical feedback and confidential advice. Along with your reputation, it's your single biggest asset. So you've got to get it right.

When seeking help, you can't assume you'll have all the right people to lean on. You can't leave it to chance. You've almost got to build it one person at a time, one conversation at a time. As a leader, employed professional or corporate executive, there are three main approaches to building out your network:

1. **Filling the Buckets**. You classify your connections as discrete 'buckets' or groups. Examples – professional, social and work. You aim specifically to add people to one or more buckets.
2. **Building the Dream Team**. You label the different kinds of people you need in your ideal network – the main players on your 'team bus'. You look at the gaps and nurture those who could take a place on the bus.
3. **Taking the RAP Route**. RAP is Random, Accelerated and Piggybacked. You build a big, varied network as fast as you can, using current connections to introduce you to their connections where you can. You go all out in the hope that you cover all the bases and you can find who you need when you need them.

Think about it. You network because you can't make the magic happen all on your own. You need to get stuff done now or in the future. You rely on others to spread the word on how well you're doing. Let's explore these three approaches in more detail so you can pick the one that works best for you.

Approach 1: Filling the buckets

Look closely at influential leaders and high-level professionals. Most manage multiple kinds of networks to help them take on more power and responsibility. When you recognize different functions for your various connections, you can begin to organize them into special buckets, groups or 'nets'. From 30,000 feet, these are:

1. **Your operational or work network**. This is your work network for getting things done day-to-day.

2. **Your professional or personal development network**. This is your personal development network for enhancing your performance.
3. **Your organizational network**. This is your strategic network for future-proofing your career.
4. **Your life network**. This is your social network to pick up everything else outside work.

Lots of networking will happen by accident. You don't really have to force the social stuff, for example. But to build a network that makes you better you must be purposeful. A hotlist of people who complement your reputation doesn't happen by accident. To grow a network that affords you career capital, you must be strategic and intentional. Networking is work after all. Otherwise it would be called 'net-eating' or 'net-socializing'. Let's explore these four 'buckets' one by one.

1. The operational network (OpNet)

This bucket of people help you get your job done. It covers your internal responsibilities and your everyday working relationships. It includes colleagues – direct reports and superiors. It might also feature outside stakeholders like clients and suppliers. You know each other well. You're focused on achieving the objectives for which you were hired.

Your work connections help you with the politics, the bureaucracy, the problem solving and the decision making. They supply ideas and resources. They help you make things happen. You don't have too much choice in who is in this network, but everyone tends to know their role in it.

In building your OpNet, it's easy to be more tactical (here's what we're doing) than strategic (here's what we should be doing). It's all about routine and the short-term demands of the job in hand. Relationships that are too fractious or close can sometimes hinder getting stuff done.

Personalities might clash. Work leaks into social. It's a rigid but necessary network. But it won't take you higher up the food chain.

2. The professional network (ProNet)

This bucket of people will help you move on and up. It's essential to facilitate any transition into leadership, authority and seniority. It gives you a wider profile outside your everyday 'internal' stuff. It develops you personally and gives you access to specialist skills

When you get to a certain stage of competence, you start to feel stifled by your work environment. You yearn for more opportunities. You feel limited by your lack of skills, knowledge and reputation. A lack of career capital is holding you back. These are signals to develop your ProNet.

Networking externally means moving outside your normal circles to increase your perspective and profile. Think alumni groups, professional associations, various committees and forums. This is often done on your own time and coin. Few people will push you do this personal networking. And few people actually build their ProNet because it takes time and effort that they don't have.

The upsides of filling this bucket are huge. The connections you make provide valuable introductions, career opportunities and insight. They may become mentors, coaches or sponsors. They help benchmark your own skills. They tell you how your career is progressing. It's a fairly safe way take your thinking and your profile up a level. And you do make yourself more valuable to your company with what you learn.

3. The strategic network (StratNet)

This bucket is very future focused. You're thinking way beyond your 'now'. Harvey McKay wrote a networking book called *Dig Your Well Before You're Thirsty*. It's a great line which stresses how important it is to think ahead about who you're going to need long term.

This StratNet is organizational in nature. It widens your horizons to the big strategic picture. It's beyond tactical and into the company's mission. The stakes are higher and the connections are higher. It takes courage to reach out. How do you add value to people who may not see the immediate benefit of even knowing you?

This kind of networking takes you into leadership territory. You reach out across functions and business units. Vertically and horizontally. You want to know what people do and where they fit into the collective. What their areas of expertise are and what they are responsible for.

When you build these relationships, you tap into the heartbeat of your organization. Every connection you make gives you more of a say in organizational strategy. As a result, you gain more executive presence because of your strategic standpoint. And you earn more career capital for future moves.

You meet more demi-gods and VIPs with this kind of networking. You're dealing with power players with significant influence. You're handling culture issues, office politics and strong personalities. This requires a higher level networking skills, greater authority and a more convincing articulation of your contribution to the cause.

4. The life network (LifeNet)

This is the obvious final bucket. It keeps what you're doing real and gives you balance in your existence. This is where your friends live. The ones you do life with, have fun with, let down your hair with, socialize with. Be vulnerable with and celebrate wins with. They are your emotional release and your sanity check.

Employers and recruiters ask the interview question *'what are your interests outside work?'* for a reason. They need to know that if work goes bad, you've got something to fall back on. Some sports, social, leisure, hobby or interest to lean into. Some perspective and support that nourishes you spiritually, emotionally and physically. If you've got nothing and your job is it, then if that goes south, your whole life goes down the pan with it.

You need friends and you also need PEAST people. This stands for Professionals, Experts, Advisors, Suppliers and Tradespeople. For when your roof leaks, your washing machine breaks down and your computer dies. For when you want to draw up a will, your daughter needs driving lessons and you need a new car.

Your LifeNet also gives you valuable support when life's trials and challenges come at you. Stress. Debt. Loss. Injury. Illness. Anger. Guilt. Parenting stuff. Health stuff. Loneliness. Indecision. Addictions. Accountability. It's tough going through all this alone. This is where best friends, community links, neighbours and even faith connections (e.g. church, mosque, synagogue) come into their own.

Applying the buckets approach

If you like the idea of seeing your networking as filling buckets, this four-pronged approach makes good sense. Be careful not to spread yourself too thinly. You've got to keep 'making plan' and bossing your every-day responsibilities. Your ProNet and your StratNet are discretionary networks. You don't build them by accident. It's intentional. It's 'over and above' your regular work. You've got to want it.

As you reach out, you're looking for some routine. Some regularity. It won't help you to dip into some higher level external networking for a 'season' then disappear back into your work cave. That's how you blow a reputation. Consistency builds trust. Familiarity builds bonds.

Try to keep business and personal separate. Be professional and do the right thing. Blurred lines can make things awkward. It's not always possible. Networks are not mutually exclusive. Take the game of golf. You can easily see how the people you meet there might cut across all four of these buckets. People leak into other networks, especially as you get to know them. People can become more useful to you as you uncover their skills.

Stay focused on your key targets. Skewing your time to people you like may be fun but not strategic. You'll need to get outside your comfort zone. Where possible, get people you know to intro you to people you don't. I call this piggy-backing. You're leveraging one network to access another.

Try always to give back. Show and share the love so people know they are valued and appreciated. Nurture your relationships and keep calibrating who you know (see later). Do most of it intentionally but leave some room for those lucky encounters and serendipitous moments. Who knows what lies on the other side of a random 'hello'?

For more insight into these kind of networks, check out:

1. *Strategic Connections* by Anne Baber, Lynne Waymon et al.
2. 'How Leaders Create and Use Networks' by Herminia Ibarra and Mark Lee Hunter.
3. 'The Three Networks You Need' by Linda Hill and Kent Lineback.

Approach 2: Building the dream team

You now understand the power of people. You need other people around you. The right kind of people. Let's call it your dream team, your team bus, your ideal network. You need the support and expertise of others who can do what you can't.

In the Dream Team Approach to defining the perfect or ideal network, you hand pick your players. You identify certain kinds of people with certain attributes and you go after them. You might already know them. You just might need to know them more. Spend time with them. Unlock their potential. See if they're really worthy of being on the team.

What follows are 16 kinds of people that you almost can't afford to be without. Some are taken from research by the Gallup Organization. This came out in the fascinating book *Vital Friends – The People You Can't Afford to Live Without* by Tom Rath. He was looking for the types of people you need in your life for maximum success and satisfaction. To find out, thousands of people all over the world were asked 'do you have a friend at work?'

I've added a few more and grouped them as follows:

1. **The Brains**. People with huge thinking capabilities, wisdom and specialist skills.
2. **The Drivers**. People who make things happen, keep you going and get things done.
3. **The Promoters**. People who talk you up, amplify your impact and multiply your connections.
4. **The Friends**. People who love you, support you and partner with you.
5. **The Critics**. People who make your life tougher, but for the better.

It's not a definitive list, as you will think of others who can help you in your situation. But it's a start. As you read through them, consider which ones you have in your network right now and where you fall short. Those are the gaps that need plugging if you're going to build your reputation and accelerate your quest for career capital.

1. The brains

These people get you thinking. They provide bold enlightenment, useful feedback and critical analysis. They help you make decisions and negotiate complex territory. Praise them and thank them for their talent and their wisdom.

- **Navigators (Mentors)**. Navigators are the friends who give you advice and keep you headed in the right direction. You go to them whenever you need guidance, and they talk through the 'pros' and 'cons' with you until you find an answer. In a difficult situation, you need a Navigator by your side. They help you see a positive future while keeping things grounded in reality. Any time you're at a cross-roads and need help making a decision, you can look to a Navigator. They help you know who you are – and who you are not. They are the ideal friends to share your goals and dreams with; when you do, you will continue to learn and grow. When you ask Navigators for direction, they help you reach your destination.

- **Mind Openers (Challengers).** Mind Openers are the friends who expand your horizons with new ideas, opportunities, cultures and people. They help you create positive change. Mind Openers know how to ask good questions, and this makes you more receptive to ideas. When you are around a Mind Opener, you are unguarded and express opinions aloud, especially controversial ones that you might not be comfortable sharing with other friends. These friends broaden our perspective on life and make you a better person. If you need to challenge the conventional wisdom or shake up the status quo, spend a few hours talking with a Mind Opener.

- **Strategists (Planners).** Strategists are skilled in planning action or policy. They are adept at office politics and accomplished in fighting wars. They are world-beating business architects. They are dynamite at converting the brainstorm and ideas into something real. Something that can be communicated and executed. They are supreme at devising your game plans and modifying it throughout the battle. They will help you coordinate your forces and play to win. If you're looking for someone to co-manage your campaign for global domination, hire a Strategist.

- **Specialists (Experts).** These are the whizzes with particular skills or knowledge. If you need particular talents to help you navigate specialist problems, bring in a Specialist. Example niche expert areas include technology, social media, presenting, negotiating, selling, culture, languages and writing. When you want to stack the deck in a key area of expertise, choose a Specialist.

2. The drivers

These people are dynamic and inspiring. They lift you up and enthuse you with their energy, ideas and positivity. They help keep you motivated and self-confident, particularly during tough times. Praise them and thank them for their passion and their all-action approach to life.

- **Builders (Encouragers)**. Builders are great motivators, always pushing you toward the finish line. They continually invest in your development and genuinely want you to succeed – even if it means they have to go out on a limb for you. Builders are generous with their time as they help you see your strengths and use them productively. When you want to think about how you can do more of what you already do well, talk to a Builder. Much like the best coaches and managers, these are the friends who lead you to achieve more each day. And great Builders will not compete with you. They figure out how their talents can complement yours. If you need a catalyst for your personal or professional growth, stay close to a Builder.
- **Entrepreneurs (Impresarios)**. These are empire builders and business owners. Sometimes inventors, sometimes ideas people. They take risks, they start things and they think big. They operate outside corporate life and bring huge business perspective. Entrepreneurs are driven, ambitious and courageous. They will push you and disrupt your thinking. They will mock your corporate existence and pity your shackled, employed routine. These are free-thinkers, free-wheelers and valuable partners. When you want out of the box thinking intelligence and audacious plans, go for an Entrepreneur.
- **Energizers (Clowns)**. Energizers are your fun friends, who always give you a boost. You have more positive moments when you are with these friends. Energizers are quick to pick you up when you're down – and can make a good day great. They are always saying and doing things that make you feel better. Energizers have a remarkable ability to figure out what gets you going. When you are around these friends, you smile a lot more. You are more likely to laugh in the presence of

an Energizer. If you want to relax and have a good time or need to get out of a rut, call an Energizer.

3. The promoters

These people are your word of mouth marketers. They want you to do well. And they're not in the habit of keeping your brilliance a secret. They have influence and power. They have reach and credibility. Praise them and thank them for their commitment to your cause and their selfless giving nature.

- **Sponsors (Patrons)**. A powerful advocate who will not just open a door for you, but will walk you through it. They are invested in developing you as a leader, often because helping your career helps theirs. They are usually a couple of levels higher than you. They have authority, influence and power. Where Mentors and Navigators give advice, Sponsors and Patrons take action. They back you and put their reputation on the line for you. They make you visible to people higher up and will almost lead you into the boardroom. When you want a high-level activist and backer who will take a bet on you, choose a Sponsor.
- **Connectors (Door-Openers)**. Connectors are bridge-builders who help you to get what you want. They get to know you and then connect you to others. These are the people you socialize with regularly. Friends who play the role of a Connector are always inviting you to lunch, dinner, drinks and other gatherings where you can meet new people. This extends your network dramatically, and gives you access to newfound resources. When you need something – a job, a doctor, a friend or a date – a Connector points you in the right direction. They seem to 'know everyone'. If you need to get out more or simply want to widen your circle of friends or business associates, a Connector can help.
- **Champions (Advocates)**. Champions stand up for you and what you believe in. They are loyal friends who sing your praises and defend

you until the end. Not only do they praise you in your presence, a Champion also 'has your back' – and will stand up for you when you're not around. They accept you for the person you are, even in the face of resistance. Champions are loyal friends with whom you can share things in confidence. They have a low tolerance for dishonesty. You can count on them to accept what you say, without judging, even when others do not. Champions are your best advocates. When you succeed, they are proud of you, and they share it with others. Champions thrive on your accomplishments and happiness. When you need someone to promote your cause, look to a Champion.

4. The friends

These people are your die-hard partners. Through thick and thin, through sun and rain, they're there for you. They love doing life with you and adore you just because you're you. Praise them and thank them for their devotion and their faithfulness.

- **Companion (Loyalists)**. A Companion is always there for you, whatever the circumstances. You share a bond that is virtually unbreakable. When something big happens in your life – good or bad – this is one of the first people you call. At times, a true Companion will even sense where you are headed – your thoughts, feelings and actions – before you know it yourself. Companions take pride in your relationship, and they will sacrifice for your benefit. They are the friends for whom you might literally put your life on the line. If you are searching for a friendship that can last a lifetime, look no further than a Companion.
- **Collaborator (Partners)**. Collaborators are people with similar interests with whom you can easily relate. You might share a passion for sports, hobbies, religion, work, politics, foods, music, films or books. In many cases you belong to the same groups or share affiliations. When you talk with a Collaborator, you're on familiar ground, and this can serve as the foundation for a lasting relationship. Indeed, in those conversations, you often find that you have similar ambitions in

work and life. Looking for someone who can relate to your passions, pastimes, projects or purpose? Find a Collaborator.

- **Enablers (Runners).** Enablers do all the mundane, unsexy stuff that allows you to be brilliant! They do the chores, the administration and the leg-work that means you can be free to do what you do best. Secretarial and support staff are classic Enablers. Along with personal advisors and specially-selected outsource partners, they take care of many of the everyday things that would just bog you down. Grandparents who look after your children while you work, spouses and partners who run the home while you're in the limelight – these are the Enablers that ensure you are free, uncluttered and empowered to do what you do better than anyone else in the world: be you!

5. The critics

These people are the pains in your behind. They set standards you strive to live up to. They crack whips, set targets and irritate you into action. Praise them and thank them for their high standards and relentless pushing.

- **Drivers (Managers).** Drivers are people who can reward you or punish you. They can incentivize you or chastise you, and sometimes you need both! Line managers and bosses often fulfil this role. Shareholders and stakeholders do likewise, as do investors and even customers and clients. You need them because they provide financial support, they have power over you and they hold you accountable for certain aspects of your personal or business life. And they give you feedback, guidelines, rules, policies, procedures and regulations that hopefully help you do a better job. When you need the rewards, the framework and the parameters to really do what you do well, your Drivers will keep you 'on task' and 'on message'.
- **Rivals (Competitors).** Put simply, Rivals make you better. Without them, you get complacent, bored, uncreative and stale. Rivals push you to innovate, to get better and to 'up your game'. They keep you sharp and wary, and encourage you to constantly develop yourself.

They can motivate you to do things differently and better, and they can even scare you into making the changes that enable you to perform at a higher level than you otherwise might. If you want to run faster, play better, deliver more, work harder, get more organized, be more creative and generally be a better you, then take notice of your rivals.

- **Role Models (Inspirers).** ~~Role Models are people you look up to, look into and admire.~~ They can be alive or dead. They can be acquainted with you personally or not. They can be famous celebrities or public figures. They can be unsung heroes. They can be aware of their role in your life or not. What they do give you is a way of living your life, a set of values, a powerful example or a lasting influence that makes you want to be like them. This is not to say you don't like being you, but that you recognize in them certain aspects, traits, characteristics, values or ways that you strive to emulate. When you need a shining example of how to deal with what you're dealing with or how to live your life, choose a Role Model.

Applying the dream team approach

Your dream team is probably already known to you. Some will already be onboard your team bus. Your challenge is playing the right people in the right positions. In assembling your dream team, here are five really useful questions to ask yourself:

1. **Who is currently fulfilling each role in your life?** You can have multiple people in each role, but obviously not too many. Check you have all the gaps covered. Some roles may be redundant for you. You might not need a Driver. Role Models might not be your thing. No need to fill it for the sake of getting all the cards in the set.
2. **Should they be in that role?** Great team managers get their players operating in their strengths. Sometimes you lean on people for the wrong reasons. You don't play to their talents. Get the square pegs in the square holes.

3. **Do you expect too much from people?** It's likely you've got a few people occupying more than one role. Beware stretching them too thinly. Sweating your assets is one thing but driving them into the ground is another. If too few people are filling too many roles, you need to enlarge your network.

4. **Who could possibly fit that role?** If you've got a gap, who could fill it? Some people in your network may be showing potential. You just need to get closer to them. Other times you've got no candidates. That means getting out there and finding them.

5. **Who is in a key role that shouldn't be there?** If you've got a gap that needs filling, you sometimes promote the wrong person. Or they end up there by default. Give them an out and let them go. They could be better deployed somewhere else. They may just need a break.

Don't be overwhelmed by the collection of personnel you need in your dream team. Just realize that, like the Avengers in the Marvel comics and films, each brings different super powers to your table. You just have to be the one who assembles the team.

A final thought on the Dream Team Approach. What roles do you fulfil in the lives of others? Where do you show up in the networks of others? You've heard the old saying 'the best way to get a friend is to be a friend'. What roles are best for you to support others? More crucially, what roles are the wrong ones for you to occupy?

Approach 3: Taking the RAP route

When building a network, most people don't leave it to chance. They think strategically about what type of help they need and from what type of person. There is another way. When you RAP your network, you go for size and speed. You're looking to make a quick impact. You'll recall that RAP stands for Random, Accelerated and Piggy-backed.

Random means you're not too precious about who you connect with at this early stage. You want to build quickly. You're going for a mile wide AND a mile deep. You're more concerned with quantity than quality. You can sift and cull later.

Accelerated means you keep momentum going. You're looking for quick wins and low-hanging fruit. You're proactive in your approaches. You're hustling. You're working it.

Piggy-backed means you use your network to build your network. You piggy-back on the connections of others to facilitate referrals and introductions. You explore peoples' networks so you know who they know. You ask for help. You cultivate the company of connectors and door openers. You see your contacts as windows into other worlds. And you take advantage.

Applying the RAP approach to networking

When you scale your connections up this fast, you usually don't have the time to judge the merits of each connection. You accept virtually all requests to connect on LinkedIn. You're open to any and all corridor conversations, social events and introductions. You think 'yes' before you think 'why'.

You may think this is similar to the Career Hustler from Chapter 1. You recall the gung-ho approach with very little strategic thinking. But you'd be wrong. This is actually a very defined strategy. Different people need different kinds of networks and different strategies at different points in their life. Perhaps for a season, this volume vs. value approach might just work for you.

Taking the RAP route gets you on the radars of all kinds of people. And quickly. It can be dangerous if you're not organized, because you'll neglect any meaningful follow up and keeping in touch. But as a short-term strategy, it works.

Summary: The networking blueprint

You can't build a reputation by being anonymous. Even if you came up with the most incredible ideas, products or insights, they would never fly. If your network is who you know, then your reputation is who knows you. You need the first to drive the second. You need a network.

Never underestimate the terrifying power of people in building your reputation. Your ability to open doors and leverage human capital is very attractive to employers. It shows you are connected, trusted and credible. It underlines your credentials to both get stuff done and gain buy in for your initiatives.

You now see the business case for networking and how your network feeds your reputation. Who you associate with says much about you. Aligning yourself with people of status, influence, power, insight, connectivity, integrity and skill is one of the most powerful reputation-building things you can do. And we know that your reputation is your single biggest contributor of career capital.

You understand the need to calibrate your network to identify gaps. It is possible to define and thus construct your ideal network. You can do it in terms of the different kinds of networks you need – the Buckets Approach. You can look at the types of people you need around you – the Dream Team Approach. And you can go fast and loose with the RAP Approach – Random, Accelerated and Piggy-backed.

All are effective. All are legitimate. All are intentional. A combination of all is valid. All will enable you to build your network wide, deep, diverse, strong and influential. You just don't know which people will be your winning lottery tickets. You may have to kiss a few frogs. But you're doing it purposefully and strategically, which will make you unstoppable.

The message is clear. Reach out strategically, authentically and even serendipitously. Yes, those chance encounters and random conversations can often be as lucrative as the planned ones. Be open to the many different ways to get you to the same goal.

Now you've got a means to distribute, amplify and support your ideas and expertise, you just need something to shout about. You need expert status. You need the Authority Blueprint ...

Chapter 5

The Authority Blueprint

'Stop worrying about what you feel like doing (and what the world owes you) and instead, start creating something meaningful and then give it to the world.'

– Seth Godin

The power of your contribution in reputation building

So, you've bought into building your network. But no amount of connectivity will help you if you have nothing to share or give. Relationships are two-way streets. People may recommend you for just being a nice person, but if there's little beyond that, your reputation is limited. You need expertise and authority. That's the difference that makes the difference. That is what you get from an Authority Blueprint.

Face it. Nothing's going to create more of a buzz around your name than you coming up with something good. Sure, who you are counts. Your integrity, your likeability, your passion. But that stuff only counts so far.

You've got to bring something else to the party. It's where you add value and contribute to the collective that signifies your worth. Your work product, your content, your ability to hit and exceed 'plan', your ideas ... these all make you worthy of respect. We call this impact your contribution, and it's your passport to a stand-out reputation.

Your knowledge, your skills and your insight all serve to make you a player to be reckoned with. Somebody worth investing in, promoting, backing. And you do that by coming up with good stuff. By making a contribution. Consistently. Reliably. Creatively.

You're going to become some kind of expert. An authority. A 'go-to' individual who comes up with the goods. This is called your contribution. It's huge career capital. The single biggest factor in building an irresistible, compelling and highly valuable reputation is your ability to make things better. That's going to take some pretty special creating. That's why we've included an Authority Blueprint. Let's explore how you do this.

Corporate environment, entrepreneurial thinking

You may have heard the career advice of seeing yourself as CEO of your own personal services company. You Inc. or something similar. There's some merit in this, but what does it actually mean to think like an entrepreneur?

Entrepreneurs turn nothing into something. There are two types, with some crossover, but we can see them all around us in many forms. First, business owners and empire builders. They build companies. They synthesize. They create. They produce. They make stuff happen. They disrupt. They refine.

Second, personal brands and experts. They build communities. They think. They write, blog, speak and create content. They have followings and fans. They are all over social media. Think of academics, online marketers, authors, speakers, coaches, consultants, trainers and gurus. They are the stand-out authorities in their fields.

What relevance does this have for today's corporate leaders, top talent and employed professionals? If you feel you can learn from what they've done to become so acclaimed and respected, then lots.

To build your reputation and your career capital, we're going to focus on the second type (personal brands and experts) to make you famous. Down the line you may break out and start your own thing. True entrepreneur style. And when you do, you'll have the capital, the reputation, the skills, the connections and the credentials. For now, let's focus on turning you into some kind of authority.

Authority is the primary way to build career capital and enhance your credentials as a leader. As a leader and thinker, your perceived authority in any field will open significant doors for you. Authority is a power statement that tells people you're a player, an influencer and an expert. A force to be reckoned with. A significant contributor to the cause.

The payoff for authority status

Make no mistake. Authority and expertise matter. They cut through noise and grab attention. They attract people to you. They create more opportunities and shorten decision-making cycles. You can push more ideas through and get things done more quickly when you are seen as an authority.

When people need what you do, you want them to come to you, above and beyond any of their other choices. Including the choice to do nothing. That's what a reputation for being an authority gives you. There's more. Authority = Reputation. You get the following major payoffs:

1. **Stand-out status**. You attract the right kind of attention from the right kind of people.
2. **Media attention**. Press and media court your comments and quotes.
3. **Influence**. Your authority and reputation goes before you and inspires people to take action.
4. **Strategic alliances**. Prominent people will want to partner with you on projects.
5. **Prestige and popularity**. People see you as 'prized'. They like what you do and share it.

6. **Premium rates**. You are worth more because you bring more to the party. You're valuable.
7. **Fulfilment**. There is a deep satisfaction in making a difference and being recognized for it.
8. **Control**. The autonomy to choose how and where you work is the ultimate authority payoff.

Sure, this is a game, but it's so worth playing. With the good name that your authority brings you, you'll lead better, play better and earn better. You'll have all the career capital you need to dictate your own terms. So few people get to do that. But just by recognising that you're in this game, you have a distinct advantage over your rivals.

Your contribution = your content

Nobody is going to wake up one day and call you the messiah of your field. Building that level of trust and credibility takes some time. It takes some serious thinking and positioning. It's a process, not a launch. It's a journey of thinking, creating, questioning, campaigning, engaging and brand building. Taking you from awareness, to loyalty and idea, to authority takes a few touchpoints. It all starts with your unique contribution.

In corporate and professional life, you can start to position yourself as an authority by creating content. Stuff that solves problems, provides insight and makes a difference. What big problem are you solving? What pain will you alleviate? What will you bring to the world? What's your big plan, your breakthrough idea, your controversial but catchy opinion? You can turn all of this into content.

Like reputation, authority isn't something you ascribe to yourself. It comes from the devotion and recognition of your tribe, community, niche or following. These 'fans' get you, rate you, believe in you and rave about you.

Authority means you're actually really good at something. It says 'your way is THE way!' You know stuff. It elevates you in your industry by sharing your distinct ideas, viewpoints and frameworks. Anyone can think and everyone has an opinion. It's only when you can distil that into a respected voice or useful methodology that you're in business. This manifests in the content you create.

Stand-out contributions are unique

Your content, your contribution – is it unique? Unique means distinctive. Being the only one of its kind. Unlike anything else. That intimidates a lot of people. Particularly people brought up in a corporate, professional environment where individuality and expression are not encouraged. You're not an entrepreneur, sure. But can you begin to think like one?

In a bland world, you only need to be a few per cent different to stand out. The world is becoming commoditized. Everything looks and sounds so similar. Gary Hamel famously said 'sameness sucks'. Corporate drones bill the required hours, hit the same targets and deliver on the same KPIs. To stand out, you need some unique take on the world. You've got to create something special.

What could be your special message, key skill, special talent, forthright opinion or big idea? What's your Unique Value Proposition (UVP) or your core competence? The most compelling game changers are found in your strengths and your uniqueness. When competitors can't copy or claim your brilliance, they can't easily follow you or stop you.

You don't necessarily need an original idea or a skill that only you possess. There were hamburgers before McDonalds. Ray Croc's take on two brothers flipping burgers in an American diner led him to create a replicable process around which he could build a consistent brand.

People don't need another Lexus, iPhone or sales technique. But they might need your variation of it. They don't need another cup to hold their coffee, or even one which keeps it hot. But one which changes colour to go with your clothes or your mood? Now you've got their attention.

You don't need to be an inventor. An architect. A designer. An explorer. Those people are not you. They don't have your skills and qualities either. They'll do it their way and you'll do it yours. Your contribution can be unique. Your content can resonate with an audience. There are lessons you can learn from how others have become authorities.

Look at the experts and personal brand entrepreneurs outside corporate life. See how they have built authority and reputation. Take what you can learn from them. Let's explore to feed your thinking on what will be your unique contribution and authority strategy.

The four types of authority

You're not likely to get promoted just for doing your job well. Because pretty much everyone else does that. That's what you're paid for. You'll get promoted because you stand out as some kind of authority or expert. You'll get hired because you've got too much career capital to ignore. Your reputation will walk through the door before you do. That's the plan. Some call it fame. We call it authority.

There are lots of ways people become famous. There are slightly fewer ways experts gain their authority. They can be roughly grouped into four areas:

1. **The Creators**. These people come up with new stuff. Or new ways of thinking about old stuff. They are thinkers and dreamers. They are inventors and makers. They initiate and originate. If you have a tendency to disrupt, you might choose the Creator route to establish your authority. The contribution of Creators is original and disturbing.
2. **The Networkers**. These people are hubs and social magnets. They create value through connecting people to information, ideas and

each other. They attract. They organize. They persuade. They convene. If you're a people person and want to become indispensable, this is your route. The contribution of Networkers is experiential and engaging.

3. **The Reporters**. These people help everyone make sense of the world. They are knowledge organizers and content curators. They report. They research. They investigate. They become the authority because of their hunger for information and meaning. If you are naturally curious and a strong communicator, become a Reporter Authority. The contribution of Reporters is expressive and meaningful.

4. **The Genius**. These people have an exceptional natural capacity of intellect. Intelligence. Ingenuity. Mental giants. Their special gifts, flair and wizardry give them distinctive character and spirit. If you feel 'special' you can stand out. You're not quite a mutant or an abnorm, but you're out there in a beautiful way. The contribution of the Genius is brilliant and passionate.

Let's go in depth into each of these four routes that you might exploit to change the world. Or at least the little part of it that you inhabit.

Authority type 1: The creator

These original thinkers and architects of life mostly use one of the following routes to make their stand-out contribution:

1. **The Anarchist**. Do you have a controversial viewpoint? American engineer W. Edwards Deming brought unconventional manufacturing methods to post-war Japan in 1950, turning them into the second most powerful economy in the world in 10 years. Don Cooper brands himself a sales heretic and deliberately messes with traditional sales BS with a refreshing way of selling. UK consultant John Seddon's prominence grew following attacks on current British management thinking. When you play devil's advocate and speak out against conventional wisdom, you'll get attention. Is there a rebel in you?

2. **The Improver.** Do you see how they might work better? Do you have a new solution to an old problem? Dr Joseph-Ignace Guillotin was a French physician who, in 1789, proposed a device to carry out less painful executions. The rest is history. A few short years ago, washrooms had hand-towels. Then hot air dryers. Then super dryers – fast and powerful. Just last week in Budapest I saw air dryers that were part of the taps. You don't need to be a full-blown inventor coming up with brand new stuff. Just look differently at the same everyday problems everyone else in your company sees.

3. **The Model-Maker.** Can you take a field or a process and weave it into a methodology or model? Any kind of prototype, system or framework to describe something can make your name. Think Stephen Covey's 7 *Habits* or Elisabeth Kubler-Ross and her *Five Stages of Grief and Loss* (denial, anger, bargaining, depression and acceptance). Think Jeff Walker's Product Launch Formula or the Eisenhower Principle of Important and Urgent Tasks. It could be as simple as 5 Steps to X or the 3 Stages of Y. It could be a diagram, a matrix or a roadmap.

4. **The Mixer.** Some people make their mark by mixing ideas and disciplines. Credit to Dorie Clark here for citing Starbucks founder Howard Schultz, who didn't invent coffee nor coffee shops. But he did bring together two ideas – American-style coffee shops and Italian coffee. With a little tweaking, viola! A multimillion-dollar global franchise. Entrepreneur Derek Halpern focuses on the use of psychology in online marketing. Have you seen chilli in chocolate? Fruit in perfume? Become seen as an authority by taking a different and valuable angle or spin on an existing topic. What could you mix to create something 10% different?

Authority type 2: The networker

These people experts know how to work a network for maximum impact. They become indispensable because everyone goes through them for one reason or another.

1. **The Maven**. Mavens are information specialists. Brilliant investigators and researchers, they know how to find information. People use them to find out what's new, what's hot and what's not. They have a direct line to new information. They accumulate knowledge, especially about the marketplace, and know how to share it with others. They have great social skills and an intricate web of communication networks to share their wealth of knowledge. They are valuable because they are information brokers. If that sounds like you, then you can make a very valuable contribution sharing and trading what you know.

2. **The Dealmaker**. These are the natural salespeople and master persuaders. They get deals over the line. They negotiate astutely and get people to say 'yes'. They have magnetism and charisma. Others find it easy to agree with them. They win things and they make things happen. If you find selling and persuading easy, you hold huge authority. Your contribution to the collective will be massive and you will never be short of opportunities. Could this be how you will make your mark?

3. **The Organizer**. Good organizers and administrators can become experts. These are the party planners and event coordinators. They book venues, get bums on seats, draw in sponsors, attract VIPs and run shows. Brilliant with people but also dynamite with the details, these people make things happen. They're also good at galvanizing a team to make an event real. If you love organizing events and people into an experience, you create the memories that make you an authority.

4. **The Connector**. These are the networking hubs and door openers who seem to know everyone. They make smart and warm introductions. Their networks cut across countries, cultures and boundaries. They have inroads into cultural, social, political and professional circles. They have a gift for seeing synergy between people. They make friends easily and have fabulous communication techniques that allow deep connections to be made in double-quick time.

They are easily liked and well trusted. They are confident, dynamic and well-organized. If you are a prolific networker, this could signify the most effective way you could contribute to your company and your cause.

5. **The Nicher.** Running any kind of community or niche makes you the authority for that audience. It could be a networking group, a Meet-Up, a LinkedIn, a Whatsapp or a Facebook group. You control and curate. You decide what gets done and what gets shown. You can monitor and regulate. You become the gate keeper and the enforcer. When you serve a small audience with specialized, targeted and relevant stuff, you quickly become an authority. There are fewer competitors so it's easier to stand out. Narrower, more specialized topics. Specific audiences with specific problems. There are so many ways to slice up a niche. Would you choose a generalist or a specialist? Pick your niche and own it. You can branch out from there, but from a position of authority and dominance. You can niche by what you do, where you do it, how you do it or who you do it for.

Authority type 3: The reporter

These people commentate. They don't really create things from scratch. They just help us make sense of what's already out there. They report. They research. They are hungry for knowledge.

1. **Researchers**. Are you a curious investigator or interviewer? Academics and journalists excel in this. But you can copy them. Brendon Burchard's Expert Academy gave huge credence to the idea that almost everybody is an expert. Even if you know nothing, you can become the 'reporter expert' by interviewing and surveying people in the know. Ask questions and test things. Find stuff out and present it in case studies, reports and white papers. Then you can say 'I've observed that … ' or 'the research shows … '. It's hard to disagree with that, and so you become the authority and the oracle.

2. **The Reviewer**. Mystery shoppers and restaurant critics are review-
ers. They give their opinion of how good something is. Could you
review books in your field of speciality? Can you appraise new software for the benefit of potential users? One lawyer attends the major
law conferences for his firm (at their expense) and brings back a
review of each one, including key learning points, a value for money
calculation and a list of key contacts made. This has built up his
reputation as a primary authority on the industry. You can review
speakers, networking events, workshops, audio programmes, blogs,
books, interviews and YouTube videos. Take your pick.

3. **The Commentator**. Are you someone who takes an interest in
the news? Perhaps a particular product, service, business function,
celebrity or department attracts your attention. Perhaps it's a field of
study, topic or theory that you could comment on. This is what people
like Seth Godin (marketing), Peter Drucker (management), Gretchen
Rubin (happiness) and John Maxwell (leadership) have done. They
look at things in a different way to other people, and make sense of it
for us. They become an authority by helping us make sense of what's
going on around us. They make the complex simple. They distil the
intricate into the simple, so idiots like you and I can understand. You
don't have to write a book, but a blog or social media commentary
would really help us mortals out. How about it?

4. **The Discoverer**. You might not spot a new star in the galaxy or a new
species of worm in the deep blue sea. But what do you see going on
that nobody else has seen? In the book *Stick – How to Change Things
When Change is Hard* the Heath brothers tell of an intern who found
that a company was purchasing 424 different kinds of gloves from
different suppliers at different prices. The same pair of gloves that
cost $5 at one factory might cost $17 at another. All types were price-
tagged and piled up on the conference table in the boardroom. You
can imagine the reaction. What can you bring to light that has perhaps been under people's noses? By seizing 'first mover advantage'
you get to bring it to your world. Because you discovered or even
uncovered it, you become the authority.

We could also have put the Maven in this group. These information specialists are data brokers. However, they're in the Networker group because of their brilliant people skills.

Authority type 4: The genius

These people are just good at stuff. It might be their forceful personality and driving passion. It could be their amazing skills and abundant talent. They do stuff that others can only dream of. And they do it without too much effort. They exude confidence in their field. They have extraordinary intellectual and creative power. It shines through in their contribution to the world.

1. **The Artist**. Do you have a well-honed skill or talent? What are you really good at that others find difficult? Practise is doing stuff over and over. To become an expert or authority in a particular skill requires time and application. It takes effort to hone your craft. Test yourself. Fail from time to time. Malcolm Gladwell's great book *Outliers* talked up the 10,000 hours skilful people spend to master their craft. It needn't take that. If you Google 'does it really take 10,000 hours to master something?' you'll get some equally smart thinkers debunking the idea. Some say 20 hours. I think of mastery as being better than 99% of the people in your space. So what are you brilliant at? Are you a geek? That's art. People who have mastered the tech stuff make the world go round. If you can boss a piece of software, a computer program, a system, a policy or procedure, a methodology, a technique ... all of these will make you the authority.

2. **The Visionary**. Have you got a big bold vision, cause or crusade? These people have a burden, a desire and a passion. They have a single-minded determination to see it through. Bill Gates wanted 'a computer in every home'. Millennial Jared Kleinart is founder of 2 Billion Under 20, a community of brilliant young things changing

the way the world thinks and works. Buy1Give1 launched in 2007 in Singapore by Masami Sato and Paul Dunn is now a global business giving initiative. When people shop, they buy two of an item and give one away. It doesn't have to be your cause. Dave Ramsey in the USA and Martin Lewis in the UK are the stand-out authorities for championing financial education. Almost every revolution starts with a lone voice. Micro improvements are okay, but quantum leaps capture imagination. If you want funding, or buy in, you might as well think big. Could you lead the charge with something huge and even outrageous?

3. **The Author**. Is there a book inside you? A topic you are deeply interested in that you want to share with the world? It takes a certain degree of talent, knowledge and discipline to write a book. Few people have it. But it's one of the very best ways to announce to the world your expert status. It's pretty easy to self-publish these days. Remember, 'authority' comes from the word author. You go deep within a topic and that makes you the ultimate source of knowledge. Give the world your take, your opinion, your interpretation of a subject and that will create a lasting reputation for you. Even if people never read the book, the fact that you've written it is hugely impressive.

4. **The Techie**. Credit to Ian Brodie for spotting how you can create an audience with new media channels and new technology. After books and journals came blogs. People who got early into blogs got lots of readers. Then YouTube, Facebook, LinkedIn, Instagram and Twitter happened. Early adopters got in at ground zero and attracted followers. In the early YouTube days, Gary Vaynerchuk published his wine reviews. He brought a whole audience into the world of wine. Check out Periscope, Blabs and Hangouts. They'll fly because it's way too crowded on the others and harder to stand out. New media brings new audiences. If you're the first to use it in your company, you'll stand out as the authority and people will beg an audience with you to find out how you made it work.

This list is not exclusive. The Reputation Toolboxes in the upcoming chapters provide lots of other ways to stand out and make your mark. But certainly these give you the best chance of becoming that stand-out expert and authority in your field or company. Create your content, your capital, your connections and your skills in these areas and you're on your way to becoming indispensable.

DCPR – the secret to a powerful contribution

Once you've got a big idea or a plan for your authority status, you've got to communicate it. To brand it, message it and take it to the world in a way that sticks, it needs to be DCPR.

- **Distinctive**. You don't necessarily need a world-changing idea or a ground-breaking new invention. You want something different enough to get noticed. Sure, the world may look and say 'I knew that already', but that should only be from delivering something existing to them in a better way. So few things are original. But we can be different and distinctive.
- **Consistent**. You've got to hold your line. Changing lanes, viewpoints, styles or topics will stop you getting traction. Being wisecracking and irreverent is a style. Being cut-throat and 'no-holds-barred' is a different one. Being austere and serious is yet another. Authority needs time for momentum to build, so hold fast to your course and stay consistent in all your branding, messaging, style, marketing and writing.
- **Passonable**. Okay, this isn't exactly a real world, but you get it. If I can't communicate your idea quickly to others, then it gets stuck at me. Transferable and passonable stuff gets shared. Quickly. And often. So stay away from deep, abstract concepts and opinions unless you're feeding a very specialized, academic audience.
- **Relevant**. You're not going to excite or even mildly interest everyone. Your thought leadership will stick and your authority build with those who resonate with your topic. If you're off message or too broad in

your scope, you're going to lose a few people around the edges. Yet polarizing an audience is good. Brands that appeal to everyone get messy and 'beige'. They end up standing for nothing. Even one of the most popular brands on the planet, Apple, alienates the army of Android fans out there!

Your network becomes your messengers

You're into prototype or beta phase. You need final sign off and a plan to take it to the world. The ideal way is through a small group of allies and enthusiasts with a vested interest in you and your work. They will take your art out there on your behalf. They'll create the first ripple that will hopefully turn into a tidal wave.

Every contribution or stellar message requires advocates and champions. You need fans and defenders. You need sales people and word of mouth marketers. Creating an army of fans or followers usually starts small. Little things can spark cataclysmic changes, but it starts with a tiny gathering.

Malcom Gladwell's awesome book *The Tipping Point* calls this 'The Law of the Few'. He gives some great examples of where crazes come from and why one idea flops and another succeeds. The book is well worth reading. Here are a couple to get you thinking:

1. **The Hush Puppies story**. At the verge of being phased out, Hush Puppies shoes suddenly become hip with a small crowd in the clubs and bars of downtown Manhattan. The shoe then appeared in malls across the world, selling millions. It had nothing to do with the company marketing. A small group of fanatics made it happen.
2. *The Divine Secrets of the Ya-Ya Sisterhood* **story**. This heartwarming, well-written book by small-time writer Rebecca Wells was

about friendship and mother–daughter relationships. After initially modest take up, it went viral, with lines of 800 people at book signings. It caught on with book clubs and reading groups. It got shared. It created a movement.

A variation of the Pareto Principle or 80–20 rule applies, where roughly 80% of the 'work' will be done by 20% of the participants. For example, in most societies, 20% of criminals commit 80% of crimes; 20% of motorists cause 80% of all accidents. With epidemics and viral videos, this becomes even more extreme with 1% of the people doing 99% of the work. Now you can't rely on the viral phenomenon above to kick-start your movement. You've got to be proactive. So who's on your team bus? Who is in your inner circle? Your discussion forum, your mastermind group, your Personal Board of Advisors?

These people will give you critical feedback and help you evaluate the feasibility of your ideas. These can be your early adopters and first-level advocates. They'll back you early and take your message out enthusiastically on your behalf. Go back to your Networking Blueprint and re-evaluate your networking strategy. Be sure you've got (or are getting) the right people around you.

Once the heavy lifting is done and your idea, product, message or skill is 'off the ground', you've got some momentum going. It's time to choose your platform.

Choose your platform

When you've got something tried and tested, or think it will at least work, then you're ready to launch. You've hopefully got a team of committed people around you to help kick-start your contribution. Still, it's not guaranteed to stick. To amplify your authority and your vision, you need a platform.

What's your mechanism for delivery? How will you scale your contribution? What are your channels to disseminate your propaganda or show off your skills? The four classic power platforms right now are videos, social media, blogs and podcasts. They get your message out there, fast and widespread.

If people can't find you, either through their existing network, social shares or through 'organic' searching, then your momentum will quickly grind to a halt. Even with a strong inner circle of influencers and 'sneezers' you still may remain a well-kept secret.

Determining the best way to disseminate your message usually means finding out where your target audience is going to be. The audience decides the platform. You've got to go where they are. I once asked the head of a global technology corporation where they network online. Her answer: 'Wherever our customers are online, that's where you'll find us too.'

It's no good having a great product and trying to sell it from a market stall in the desert. No traffic. No buyers. Cal Newport's research cleverly found out that remarkable ideas (those worthy of being remarked upon) need a place or delivery mechanism to be talked about. Hence *you've got to be findable*. Secrecy and authority don't play out well together for personal brands and influential leaders.

Select and grow your audience

A great message or killer contribution is only half the picture. You're looking for an audience. A hungry crowd for whom you will provide enlightenment. These are the people who are most interested in and most receptive to your message. They are usually the ones who will benefit the most from who you are, what you have to say or what you can do.

In a sense, all leaders are thought leaders. Those you command are interested in your opinions. So your closest and most accessible audience will be your colleagues and bosses. But for the best career capital and reputation, you need to go wider than that. Outside your office, your corridors and your building. Out across the company and the industry. Up to the boardroom and down to the mailroom. In your location, region, state and country. Then to the world.

It sounds grand, but it can happen. Your message will spread out through your early advocates and your close associates. It will also come in through being found, principally online. If you are searchable on Google and social media, then you can really build a tribe.

Building a tribe is the ultimate goal for any serious career builder. Through engagement, listening and nurturing, you can turn your audience into a committed following. The magic happens when your fans and followers talk to each other. This creates leverage and creates a community of which you are the hub, the authority, the leader and the catalyst.

There are so many examples of this. You'll already be in the tribe of various authors, writers, experts and thought leaders whose stuff you love engaging with. You've already got your favourite gurus and thinkers whose voice and content you really relate to. None of them started out with an audience of millions. They started at ground zero.

Authorities and experts are largely ordinary people just like you and me. They've just had the discipline, the strategy and the entrepreneurial spirit to (a) make a difference and (b) tell their story. If you can do that, even on the smallest of scales, you'll embark on a journey of influence, reputation and opportunities that 99% of career professionals only dream of.

Thought leadership comes from content

The crucial first ingredient for sharing your brilliance (besides trying to assemble your personal network) is content creation. Content is your premium currency for establishing your authority and showcasing your contribution.

Valuable, sharable content attracts people to your thoughts, ideas and intentions. It demonstrates your expertise in a way people can see with their own eyes.

Despite the sheer amount of noise and information overload, the currency for authority remains content. You've got to put something out there. And when you do it in the right way to the right audience, you'll hook enough to create a following.

You're not just adding your voice to the noise for the sake of it. Not just another blog post or tweet. Content is king but it must be good content. Content that helps people make sense of their situation. Helps them solve problems.

This is the realm of thought leadership. The intentional creating and sharing of content that showcases your big idea or your authority. It comes from your 'platform' and presents your take on your slice of the world. Even if the audience is small, they'll go through the stages of awareness, education, engagement and sharing with others.

People won't find or share what isn't there. When you start creating content, it will get picked up in a couple of ways. One, people will discover it themselves through searching. Two, they'll find it through other people sharing.

People naturally share stuff. It's in our nature. We share stories, experiences, great products and services, interesting ideas. So take advantage of this. Listen, there are no magic bullets, magic wands, magic pills. It's down to you and up to you. Get creating content. Make it relevant, findable and good. And while you carry on developing your skills, ideas and career capital, the world will soon get to hear about it.

Summary: The authority blueprint

It's not good enough to be just good. You've got to be seen to be good. This requires a contribution of epic 'go-to' proportions. By thinking entrepreneurially (creating something from nothing) you gain a passport for promotion.

Your contribution is that idea, that insight, that work product, that message that signifies the value you bring to the corporate party. It's got to be a little better or different. And passonable. Remarkable stuff gets remarked upon. It must point to your 'stand-out' authority status.

When you do this, the payback is huge. All kinds of great benefits accrue to you, from faster career progression to greater career options. From perks, pay and interesting projects to career kudos, choice and control.

There are many ways to become that authority figure. You really only need one! Work on your skill, your art, your content. If you don't practise and really get good, you won't make your mark. You're going to be an expert, a thought leader. That requires some serious thinking and communicating.

Start on your road to stardom with some early adopters. This is your network, your inner circle of fans and messengers. Advocates who are willing to help kick-start your movement. Get your platform right with the medium that will best disseminate your brilliance. Your audience will then start to grow and the magic starts.

You're off and running. You're connected. You're creating. You're making a contribution and you're becoming an authority. You've done the heavy lifting. You've broken the back of building a 'go-to' reputation.

It's time for the icing on the cake – your four Reputation Toolboxes. You'll dive deep into specific ways to build your profile and visibility, your positioning and authority, your professional 'on the job' performance and your own Personal Board of Advisors.

These are your keys to unlock a formidable, extraordinary reputation that will make it easy for others to promote you and protect you. Over 150 ways to build significant career capital and grow your reputation as the authority and most promotable person in your space.

The four Reputation Toolboxes are the meat on the bones. They'll bring you the Holy Grail of work you love on your terms. When you get that, you've won the Career Game!

Part Two

The Four Reputational Toolboxes

'A good reputation is more valuable than money.'
– Publilius Syrus

This is the business end of the book. The practical side of things. Where you execute. You've learned about it and dreamed about it. You've made some plans and got some direction. Now you're going to action it.

There is no one way to stand out in a crowd. There is no one way to create career capital or build a reputation. You need a few approaches that play to your strengths, your style and your endgame.

Coming up for you are four Reputation Toolboxes. These are the 'how to' part of your reputation. They give you specific ways you can build career capital, raise your profile, position yourself as the expert in your field and distinguish yourself professionally from your competitors. The four tool-boxes are:

1. **PROFILE**. Keyword – VISIBLITY. Gives you ways to get your name out there and appear on the radars of influential people
2. **POSITIONING**. Keyword – AUTHORITY. Gives you ways to estab-lish your credentials as the expert in your space
3. **PERSONAL BOARD**. Keyword – NETWORK. Helps you choose and leverage your own Personal Board of Advisors
4. **PROFESSIONAL**. Keyword – PERFORMANCE. Helps you develop continually, professionally and personally to build 'on the job' cred-ibility.

Everything here creates career capital that you can trade up for more career choice and work you love. All of them will build your reputation, the single biggest and most critical of your career capital weapons.

In the following chapters, you'll get an explanation of what each one means, then a checklist of tactics you might want to deploy in that toolbox. Remember: play your own game to your own strengths. Your weapons are not mine. You'll do it in a different way to me. Why? Because you're wired up differently. You've got different talents and qualities. You find things easy that I find difficult. And you've got different career objectives in dif-ferent environments. So do it your way. It's the best way.

How to use the four reputation toolboxes

Where can you have the biggest impact in the shortest possible time? Once you begin to crack this, you can move on to others. Reputations are built over time. As you read through all of the tips, remember that you can do anything but you can't do everything. So don't feel overwhelmed by the list.

There are over 150 ideas and suggestions here. You just need a few. Don't go crazy. You don't need to be brilliant today. Just a bit more brilliant than you were yesterday. As you go through each toolbox, pick two or three that you like based on the following three criteria:

1. **Current**. Which of these do you already have a head start with? You're already a good way down the road. You're showing up for them right now, so it's a case of doing them more or more intentionally. Find out what good things people are saying about you currently. If you've already got a track record or a reputation in a few key areas, and you know it will help you down the line, build on what you've got. Otherwise you're just starting again from the ground up. Which is okay if you really have to.
2. **Aspirational**. Which of these attract you? Which would you like to be known for? Which have you always thought you'd like to get more into? Looking ahead, what do you want to be known for that you're currently not? If you've had any kind of negative or neutral reputation in the past, which of these would you like to replace that with?
3. **Strengths**. You can start fresh with these, but you'll get better and faster results taking action in an area of strength. It's no good saying you're going to be super punctual and reliable if you've never before shown those qualities. It's going to be too tough for you. Leave that to other people and play where you know you can make up some ground.

To begin with, maybe select a few that are easy wins for you. Enjoy the journey. There should be something in here to spark your enthusiasm and make you see that this is possible for you. You're taking control. You're having a say. You're playing the Career Game and with the formidable 'go-to' reputation you're building, you're going to win!

Overview 1 – Your PROFILE toolbox: Visibility

You might be competent in your job and have some great ideas. But who is seeing that? It's important that you somehow let the world know how great you are. Call it personal marketing, ethical bragging, profile raising or shining your light. Your incredible feats and skills are no good to you if nobody knows about them.

This is why you need to lift up your profile for people to see. Through a blend of writing, speaking and networking, you've got to take your brilliance out to the world. Your keywords here are visibility, connections and prominence. The PROFILE toolbox helps you answer the following questions:

- To whom does your work matter?
- Who are you trying to influence?
- Who do you need on your team?
- How can you reach them and engage them?
- How do you build a formidable network?

This toolbox equips you to identify your target audience and reputational stakeholders. You'll get lots of strategies and approaches to get on their radars and build relationships with them. You'll no longer be a great secret. The more people you know, the more people know of you. Remember: your network is who you know. Your reputation is who knows you.

Overview 2 – Your POSITIONING toolbox: Authority

You might be professionally capable and well connected. But you still have to position yourself properly to develop a world-class reputation. To become *extra special*, you have to be doing the stuff that your rivals are not doing. So craft your message or your big idea. Define your contribution to the cause and the company.

Decide what's going to make you stand out and how you'll differentiate yourself in a competitive career marketplace. The keywords here are content, contribution and authority. The POSITIONING toolbox helps you answer the following questions:

- What do you want to tell the world?
- How will you make the difference?
- How can you become an authority in your space?
- How do you position yourself as the number-one choice?

When you position yourself as any kind of expert, you develop authority status. By putting great stuff 'out there'. You've got to be making a tangible contribution offline (face to face) and online. So this toolbox will show you the different ways to become an authority and a thought leader.

Be seen as an expert. Craft your outstanding contribution or big idea. As a result, your requests for help, support, pay raises, control, choice, freedom and meaning in your work will be gladly received.

Overview 3 – Your PERSONAL BOARD toolbox: Network

This is about making the most of your connections to further your career goals. The most powerful way to do that is by assembling your very own Personal Board of Advisors (PBA) or Directors. These will be your battle HQ. Your mastermind group. Your inner circle of influence.

Your relationships are a critical factor in finding and landing work you love on your terms. The keywords here are leverage, network and advocates. The PERSONAL BOARD toolbox helps you answer the following questions:

- Who is best equipped and most motivated to help me?
- Who can elevate my reputation most if I associate with them?

- How can I best leverage my connections?
- Who are the best advocates and sponsors for me and my personal brand?

You won't do this alone. All the networking, speaking and writing you do to raise your profile is going to create valuable connections. You must decide what to do with these people. Where are they fitting into your grand plan?

You'll see clever ways to leverage those connections to bolster your career capital. You'll get lots of insight into putting together your PBA. You'll get tips on managing your contacts and leveraging your network and smart ways to add value so that these VIPs and demi-gods want to help you.

Overview 4 – Your PROFESSIONAL toolbox: Performance

This toolbox is all about your accomplishments in your everyday work. It gives you a ton of great tips and strategies to build your 'on the job' reputation. The keywords here are performance, delivery and credibility.

Get the basics right. Do your job well. Hit your targets. Make plans. Deliver over and above what's expected of you and you'll soon begin to stand out in the crowd. The PROFESSIONAL toolbox helps you answer the following questions:

- How can you stand out in your day-to-day job?
- What will get people talking about you on a daily basis?
- How do you ensure you constantly keep creating career capital?

Competence at work is a qualifier for promotion. It gets you in the game. It gets you considered. But it's not a differentiator, since pretty much everyone is competent. You need credibility, a 'best in class' performance and a high standard of delivery. Any combination of three to five items in this Professional Toolbox will do this for you.

Chapter 6

Your Profile Toolbox: Visibility

'A successful reputation is built on the three pillars of visibility, credibility and then profitability.'

– Dr Ivan Misner, Founder of BNI and *NY Times* bestselling author

Visibility – connections – prominence

This thrust of your reputation building focuses on raising your profile so you're not the world's best-kept secret. The three best ways to be more prominent are speaking, writing and networking.

If you're going to become any kind of authority or stand-out candidate for promotion, you must elevate your profile, your visibility and your presence. This will get you onto the radars and into the mobile phones of the right people. You've got to know and be known.

Dr Ivan Misner, Founder of Business Network International, created a wonderful VCP Process® for networking and reputation building. I've always liked this model because it puts all of your relationship building and profile raising into a logical sequence. First you have to be visible, so people see you. It's no good being brilliant but anonymous. Very few people have changed the world by being a well-kept secret.

Then you have to be credible, so people value you and 'buy' you. If they don't rate you or your ideas, you'll never be talked about. Then your personal brand becomes profitable, so people sell you and recommend you.

The overall message is **be everywhere that counts**. Familiarity and visibility drive reputation. Throw your net wide. Be consistent. You can't dip in and out of things. You've got to keep showing up. We'll go into specifics in this toolbox, where you'll find over 40 ways to boost your visibility. Get out there. Make connections. Be there in person and in writing. Don't be a secret!

1. Court your local media

It actually doesn't take as much as you think to get into your local press. Think of your local or regional papers and magazines. Think of your local TV and radio stations. National coverage may be harder, but they generally pick their feeds up from local stations anyway. The word to remember is 'stories'.

All news outlets are looking for great local stories featuring local people. There are now so many channels on television and radio that producers often don't have enough guests to fill their air time. That's where you come in!

These people need credible comments and analysis on the many different events that take place every day. You've got insight and knowledge, opinions and solutions, stories and lessons. So why shouldn't that expert be you? Your job is to find an angle.

If they come to you for quotes and interviews, say 'yes'. And keep saying yes. Publicity is profile. Develop good relationships with journalists in your area. Make sure they know:

- Your particular areas of expertise.
- What kind of people, situations or topics you can add valuable insight to or comment on.
- Your availability and contact details.
- Your other contacts so they come through you to source experts and influencers.
- How reliable and responsive you are.
- You are available to write articles, comment on stories and supply quotes.

Don't underestimate your opinion. You've got a take on local happenings. You have a view on how national and international news affects locals. You have comments, insight and contributions about key life and business issues.

You have great stories to tell about how you got started in your role or where your 'big idea' came from. You've got tales of overcoming adversity. Success stories. Examples of how you, your company, your product or your service has made a difference. Are you getting the idea?

To check whether your story is viable for radio, television or press, have a look at the news over the next few days. Particularly the local news. Is what you've got to say at least as interesting as any of those pieces? Of course it is. You just need an 'in' to win some valuable air-time. Be proactive in suggesting angles and stories for them. They'll soon be coming to you for contributions.

2. Write a blog

This is short for a web log. It's basically your take on a topic. It's a great reputation-building tool for employed professionals, leaders and executives. If you don't have a company website to plant it on, use LinkedIn. You can post all of your content on there if required. With a few hundred million members worldwide, you're bound to get some eyes, some shares and some likes.

Blogs are a powerful way to share your ideas, projects and opinions. They provide a shop window for your thought leadership in a way that talking doesn't. They're a permanent record of your brilliance. They're also a useful hub to direct people to which underlines your credentials.

If you get into blogging, be regular. A post every few months won't really do much for your personal brand. Create a list of 20–30 topics or titles you could write about. Over the next six months. Pledge to do one a week and see what happens to your reputation.

3. Write professional articles and guest blogs

As well as your local press, look for opportunities to write for trade journals and professional publications. Add newsletters and online websites to that list. All need great content to make them interesting. Writing pre-sells others on your abilities, and exposes you to thousands of prospects. Remember the word 'author' has the same root as 'authority'. You are the source!

There's nothing quite like having your name in print to differentiate you from others that do what you do and give you that extra level of respect. You'll gain kudos from people that already know you and you'll gain attention from people that don't yet know you. Both avenues are vital in building your reputation as the number one 'go-to' choice for what you do.

4. Respond to blogs and intranets

You may not be the most creative writer, but it doesn't take much to remark on other people's writing. A smart way to raise your profile is to comment on other people's posts. You can encourage, compliment, agree with, add to or even disagree with.

Any interaction is usually appreciated, as it shows the world their stuff has been read and hopefully enjoyed. It stimulates conversations and of course makes you memorable. This is an especially effective way to get onto the radars of influential people, particularly those outside the company.

5. Write a book

A book is a great reputation building tool! I'm not talking about Harry Potter type stuff, but solid, non-fiction in your area of expertise. You can get a Word doc turned into a book and get the book cover designed for a few dollars on fiverr.com. There's no excuse not to.

It doesn't have to be a huge book; 10,000 words would make a decent read. You won't make millions from it. In fact, you won't even sell it. You'll give it away as a 'business card on steroids' book. What a huge added value networking gift!

It needn't be an original work. It can just be your take on a problem; your view of a topic. It's uniquely yours. And totally doable. Writing a book will give you three things:

- It raises your profile.
- It's an excellent marketing tool.
- It's a fabulous way to share your expertise and knowledge.

They say that when it comes to writing a book, it's not what the book makes for you, it's what the book makes of you. It's the person you become in writing it. You gain greater knowledge, more confidence from the sense of accomplishment and increased discipline in actually writing the thing. And it's who you become in the eyes of others as an authority.

6. Create special reports, white papers or guides

Almost anything you write makes you an authority. Even if people don't read it, the fact that you've written something creates credibility. What topic, problem, trend or idea could you write something about? Here are a few ideas to get your creative juices going:

- *The 10 Biggest Mistakes Made By* _____
- *7 Things You Need to Know About* ___
- *5 Ways* ___ *Will Affect* ___ *This Year*
- *12 Ways to Get More* _____
- *9 Reasons to* _____
- *How to* ____

Sounds like Scott's VPs

They can be just a page or two. But you'll soon build up a body of work that will do wonders for your profile.

7. Say 'Yes' to more things

All huge personal brands start small. You've got to be courageous and adventurous. Raise your hand when opportunities, assignments and schemes come up. Find out what projects, ventures, initiatives and event plans are happening. See if they need any support or help. If they ask you a few times and get 'no' after 'no' then they'll stop asking.

8. Show up

Lots of people say 'yes' to stuff, only to bail out. They plan to go networking. They promise to create some content or write a blog. They just don't show up. They say commitment is doing what you say you're going to do, even if you don't feel like it.

Be someone that shows up. Someone who takes part and gets involved. If you say you'll be there, be there. Even if you're not in the mood. You can't build a profile by not being visible. Do what many others won't. Show up. Every time you do that, you add another chunk of social and career capital to your store.

9. Attend TEECCS

This stands for trade-shows, expos, exhibitions, conferences and conventions. These are big regional, national or international external events with huge networking opportunities. Choose 6–10 key business events over a 12-month period. Get the company to fund everything given that you'll be returning with valuable 'bring back'. This describes valuable learning, connections, opportunities and insight that will benefit your organization. This could take the form of:

- introductions you make to your colleagues
- useful literature
- training materials
- an executive summary or presentation
- insider knowledge or useful trends
- potential partners, customers or clients.

Attendance at these events keeps you connected to all the people, knowledge and trends you need to be held in high repute. You also get the opportunity to raise the company's profile in the wider industry. The networking opportunities at events such as these are huge. Whether you exhibit or not at these trade shows, you can make some excellent contacts and pick up important business cards.

Many such events now have guest speakers and seminars, which are great places to spend your time and network with the good and the great. Conferences are equally valuable in personal marketing terms. Remember: you can build a reputation by association.

10. Sign up for BPCFs

BPCF stands for boards, panels, committees and forums. Gatherings such as these give you great opportunities to network with new contacts and to showcase your talents. They will also get your name on research papers, reports, press releases and official documents. You'll become a key person of influence.

Bodies such as these have decision-making powers. They dictate policy, drive strategy, shape events and build consensus. They have the inside track on what's really happening. They give you a platform for change and a channel of influence. If you're serious about building your reputation and enhancing your good name with the right people, then signing up for these kinds of opportunities is your fast-track way to achieve it.

Search out people who are already on such boards and committees, and ask them if they'd appreciate more help. It's usually always a 'yes'. When you're established on there, you may even have the power and influence to bring on your own advocates and friends.

11. Do interviews and research

An easy way to get 20 minutes with a demi-god or VIP in your company (and sometimes outside) is by interviewing them. When you make the ask for them to get involved, remember to give them a compliment first, perhaps saying why you chose them. A few scripts:

- *I'm doing a piece of research into _____. You've got a great reputation for ___ and I'd love to get your thoughts on it. Can you spare 15 minutes on the phone over the next couple of weeks?*
- *I'm interviewing a few high level leaders to get their thoughts on _____. You've always been outspoken in this area and I've admired your passion and insightful comments. Would you be open to a 30-minute interview at your office sometime over the next month?*

You get the idea. The added bonus is that you'll offer to share the findings with them. This gives you another excuse to go back to them and perhaps get more time with them.

12. Teach at a local college or university

With your business expertise, you can offer much to the local students who are studying enterprise, entrepreneurship and business. An occasional lecture or teaching slot will offer you status as an expert and enhance your reputation.

You'll gain new contacts. You'll get something amazing and distinctive to put on your LinkedIn profile and your résumé. Who knows what other opportunities it might lead to? Your current employers should see merit in you raising the profile of the company by dedicating yourself to advancing the local student population.

13. Join professional associations, clubs and organizations

Joining professional associations gives you a chance to shape policy, get ahead and be a part of new ideas. This is a great way to broaden your network, raise your profile and gain valuable external perspective. It allows you to influence, and certainly raises, your profile. There are many professional bodies and associations that represent every industry and sector.

If you want to raise your profile in your industry, there's often nothing better than joining one or more professional groups or clubs. Better still, are there opportunities to serve on committees and boards there? It's great for your résumé and will give you a wealth of experience in your field. That's what builds a reputation!

14. Get your own website

If you're allowed to, get your own website. Employed people in corporate and professional roles can gain huge kudos by having their own site. It showcases them as individuals and creates huge prominence. It might just be a one-page blog site. Easy to do in an hour if you know someone who can show you how.

You'll need to find a good domain name. It doesn't need to be a '.com' ending. There are loads of great 'suffixes' now, so you should be able to get your name in their somewhere. That's a crucial point. Try to use your name rather than something generic like www.project-management-thoughts.com or similar. You can publish your own articles and books on your site, and share your views with blogs and comments.

15. Get on social media

A huge one this. So obvious too, and worthy of a whole book. But you already know the power of social media in your visibility and profile. If you're good at what you do, you need to identify every possible way of being 'out there'.

What's the use of people knowing who you are and how great you would be for them if they can't remember your name, have mislaid your email address or can't find you on Google?

It doesn't matter too much what platform you're on in the early stages. Twitter, Instagram and Facebook are pretty accepted commercially. The problem a lot of people have with social media is wasted time. This is usually through a lack of strategy and understanding of how it all works.

No question it's a powerful profile-raising tool, so check it out. Hang out with a friend or two that really get it, and learn what they know. You could even hire somebody or outsource to a specialist to handle your social media stuff for a few bucks a month.

16. Promote your image

How can you get your photo out there more? It's not as good as you being there, but it keeps a visual in front of people. Instead of text stuff on social media updates, can you be more camera-savvy? Can you get into Instagram and share some good (but professional) images of you? Can you get more shots taken with people in your network to share with others?

Images are powerful reinforcers of brand. They stick in people's minds. People will see you more, remember what you look like and thus remember you more. Your image on a business card is great if you are allowed to do it. Be visible in name and visible in face. That's a reputational double whammy!

17. Get photographed with influential people

Who you hang around with says much about who you are. Appearing alongside demi-gods in photographs is a great boost for your reputation.

These images can appear on your own social media outlets. They might also show up on channels and sites that are not yours. This exposes you to an even wider audience. As an upside, when you get alongside important people, you change your viewpoint and start moving with higher level people.

18. Share what you're doing

There's a double whammy benefit of getting out there networking. One is doing it. Another is telling people about it. If you're going to an industry event, put it out there on social media or the company intranet. Tell a few people. Mention anybody you're going with. This 'bigs up' your connections too.

It doesn't have to just be networking events. It could be a project you're working on or some writing you're doing:

- *Excited to be attending the XYZ conference in _____ with Tim Jones.*
- *Just booked onto the _____ seminar. Who else is going?*
- *Just preparing my presentation on _____ for _____. #Excited*
- *Writing a white paper on _____. Any thoughts on what should be in there?*
- *Looking forward to interviewing the legendary Tim Jones on the topic of _____. What should I ask him?*

You get the gist. It's all great engagement. Plus you're raising your profile by keeping your name out there. When you look busy, people think you're popular, active and in demand. All good for your reputation.

19. Set goals for profile-raising activity

You can't afford to leave your reputation to chance. Set small, achievable goals for things like networking, content creating or social media. These can be daily, weekly or monthly. Some examples:

- Reach out to a minimum of 50 people per month, either by phone or email.
- Make 5 social media posts a day.
- Make 10 phone calls before 10 am, 3 days a week.
- Go to 3 networking events a month.
- Write a blog a week.
- Write a white paper this month.
- Do one interview a month.
- Connect to 5 people a day on LinkedIn.

These small, cumulative actions add up to huge visibility. Soon you'll be everywhere and people will think you're a mover and shaker in your world.

20. Get your name right

If you want 'front-of-mind' awareness to distinguish you from the rest, then get your name right. If you've got a famous name, can you use a middle initial or variation of it? My name, Rob Brown, is the same name as a Hollywood actor. He's not an 'A' list celebrity but he's famous enough to come up when people Google 'Rob Brown'. Makes me work harder to be 'up there' when people search for me.

My social media profiles use *TheRobBrown* (as in 'the one and only Rob Brown') to create some differentiation. One friend with my name actually uses Rob P Brown to distinguish himself from me! If you're in this situation, you'll need some variations of your name to help you distinguish yourself.

21. Beef-up your email signature  (Personal)

What does your email signature say? Can you 'beef it up' a bit? Rather than the boring standard ones, see if you can add any of these:

- A photo of you?
- A project you're working on?
- An interesting job title?
- A link to your recent blog post.
- An invitation to your next event.
- Your latest social media post.

Not only do you come across as someone a bit different, you do the stuff that few others are doing. Email sigs are seen hundreds of times a day. See if you can make yours work harder for you. In fact, your goal is to make people specifically comment on it. Internally, externally or both!

22. Send out a newsletter

Would a monthly newsletter or regular e-shot help your reputation cause? Even with 50 interested recipients, it keeps you front of mind. You could share great websites, valuable tips, useful resources and helpful ideas to your carefully chosen target audience. A monthly catch-up email to a few friends and colleagues can grow to a substantial audience.

On a scaled down level, a simple thing such as sharing the occasional clean joke, funny email, motivational quote, interesting story or useful link can keep you in front of people and remind them you're around. You're making people smile, which is no bad thing when it comes to building a reputation.

23. Speak publicly

How good are you at presenting? There are many organizations and associations that you could offer your services to as an expert. Given most people fear speaking in public, it's a great way for you to stand out.

You could also develop your presentations in team meetings, staff briefings, product launches and sales pitches. Presenting and speaking sets you up as an authority. It gives you prominence as you're the expert. You also leverage your time and your impact as you're reaching out to many people at the same time. Whether it's to small audiences and meetings, or larger conferences and seminars, actively search out and fill opportunities to address an audience.

If you really want to build your reputation quickly and emphatically, find an audience, craft a compelling message and address them with your insight and passion. That may mean conquering your fear of speaking, but there are lots of great trainers, courses and tips out there to make you better.

24. Tell repeatable stories

How good are you at telling stories and jokes? Good ones get repeated. Hopefully with your name somewhere in there as the source or subject. Telling stories is a skill you can learn. It helps you spread your messages and also helps you in presentations.

25. Run your own event

Few things put you at the hub of a group of people better than organizing an event. Magda was a student course representative and was already building her reputation as a spokesperson for her subject area. When she decided to put on a one-day conference on a Saturday to bring all 8898

course reps together, she gained huge experience, massive visibility and crucial air-time. Some ideas:

- a social event
- a discussion group
- a panel Q&A
- a networking event
- a seminar or conference
- an after-work get together
- a sporting competition
- a party
- a movie
- a lunch
- a meal after work
- a long distance Skype group video chat.

Most of these wouldn't take much organizing. Some are obviously a bit more involved. All of them would give you huge prominence, particularly if you invited some VIPs and influencers. What could you do to bring people together with you in the middle?

26. Do some co-promotion

You might not need (or be able to afford) a publicist to help you regularly comment on important issues in your field. But you can work with a wingman or co-promoting colleague who also wants to raise their profile. This works on the idea that what people say about you is often more influential than what you say about yourself.

So next time you go networking or to a conference, partner up with a friend or colleague. Pledge to look for opportunities for one another. Talk each other up if you meet anyone interesting that should know about them.

They'll hopefully do the same about you. It's often easier complimenting and promoting somebody else than doing it for yourself.

27. Be the spokesperson

Anytime you're working on a project with people, volunteer to be the one who feeds back. It may mean extra work, but if you do the presentation or talk through the report, you'll get the profile and the career capital.

Any opportunities to talk or present to groups, you should take. If it scares you, take it. If it's to senior, influential people, take it. Speaking is a powerful profile raiser and visibility creator. Every opportunity to present publicly gives you huge career capital. Even if your presentation skills are not properly honed yet, people will admire you for trying. Plus you'll get valuable practise for next time.

28. Study the org chart

Find out who the movers and shakers are in your company. Look across disciplines, functions and departments. Look up and look down. Identify the key players and get on their radars. This could mean bumping into them or knocking on their door and introducing yourself. You could reach out to them on social media or get somebody who knows you both to introduce you. The org chart is a great tool for mapping out a network and ensuring you're known by the people that count.

29. Get around the right people

Your peers, your colleagues, your friends and your family help to define you. The best reputations in the world can be undermined by ill-chosen connections and poorly managed relationships. Who you associate with says a lot about you and your reputation. You become the company you keep.

People will judge you by the people you hang around with. Ensure those people fit with your desired reputation. In analysing who might be adversely affecting your reputation, ask yourself 'is the juice worth the squeeze?' Sometimes you need to let people go. Both because they are not good for your reputation and to make room for more of the right people.

30. Befriend the door openers

Who do you know that knows everyone? These people are worth knowing. They open doors to networks you could never reach without them. Go out of your way to look after these people, buy them coffees, big them up to others and invite them to things. They will be powerful allies for you in your quest for visibility.

31. Get to KFC

Not the obvious. KFC in this context stands for kitchens, fountains and corridors. The suggestion is to make the most of those impromptu chats in your office. Be open to chatting a little during those everyday encounters.

Linger a little in public places and you'll soon be involved in some good conversations. Some might be gossip, which is always handy for staying abreast of the office politics. Beyond that, all kinds of great relationships and connections start out of a chance meet up next to a coffee machine.

32. Go door knocking

Who needs to know you in your building? How about just knocking on their door one time and saying something like ...

- *Hi I was just passing and realized we'd not met before. Just wanted to introduce myself really quickly.*

- *Hi sorry to interrupt you. I was looking for Tim's office. I don't believe we've met before. I'm ____.*
- *Hi, just wanted to say a quick hello. I'm new here so I'm just introducing myself to a few people and making some new friends.*

This takes some courage, but who knows what might come of it. You'll certainly be on the radars of a few more people.

33. Start a KIT marketing file

KIT stands for keep in touch. Trouble is most people don't do it very well. The two biggest reasons people fail in this area is they're not organized enough and they don't know what to say. A KIT marketing file gives you reasons to connect.

All you do is create a couple of folders to collect good stuff you come across. Make one online, using a program like Evernote. And the other offline, in a draw or cabinet. Cut out articles in papers and magazines. Collect quotes, email funnies (clean ones!) and good ideas. Send with a simple 'saw this and thought of you … ' for a great impact.

You can leverage your collected collateral by sending the same article to multiple people. If it's a hard copy, just photocopy it. As long as you personalize the message, it's powerful way to keep in touch and add value at the same time.

34. Follow up diligently

Most people don't follow up after networking. There are many reasons for this. You could be too lazy or disorganized. Maybe you don't know what to say or how to do it. Perhaps you just don't see the point. We've done a Follow Up Manifesto for you in the Reputation Vault. It gives you lots of useful tips for following up and keeping in touch after you've met someone. Three quick follow up tips for now:

- **Strike quickly**. If you don't follow up soon after meeting someone, they'll forget about you.
- **Use different approaches**. You've got phone, email, text and social media to make a follow up connection. Choose the one where they are most likely to respond.
- **Get organized**. Plan follow up time in your diary else it will probably never happen.

To stand out, sometimes all you need to do is what other people won't or don't do. Following up with your relationships is a great differentiator and profile raiser.

35. Eat and drink more

This may look odd, but one of the best networking techniques is to ensure you don't eat and drink alone. Taking someone with you for coffee or having lunch with a contact means you're networking constantly. Even if the someone you want to build a relationship with can't come out with you, bring them something back. It keeps you on their radar and makes them remember your generosity.

36. Get sporty

Use sports, hobbies and leisure as a way to connect with people. Find out what people are doing inside and outside work by way of recreation, and find some common ground. Could you start a jogging or walking club at work? A bowling gang or a soccer game? Sport unites.

It needn't be so active. War games, chess, backgammon, computer games, book clubs, golf, swimming … the list is endless. You can kill two birds (social and work) with one stone (play together) and do some great networking.

37. Volunteer

Volunteering raises your profile, because very few people do it. Ideally, lead a team of volunteers, because it will develop your leadership skills in a way that normal business never can.

There are hundreds of volunteering opportunities within a 10-mile radius of your house! Ask others what they've done and who they might recommend to talk to about getting involved. As well as feeling good about helping, volunteering bolsters your résumé. You also get to connect to terrific people you otherwise might not meet. And that's great for your reputation.

38. Recommend people

A brilliant way to get on people's radar is to do them a recommendation, testimonial or endorsement. LinkedIn is great for something like that because it's public and visible. You can do it out of the blue. You'll be front of mind when they see it and front of mind when they connect with you to thank you.

Identify 20 people who you'd like to compliment over the next month. Give some thought as to why they're good and what you like about them. Not only is it a wonderful 'give' to big people up like this, it's also something they'll remember for a long time. Great for your reputation.

39. Talk behind people's backs

Let's say you wanted to get onto the radar of Tim Jones. A smart way is to get around somebody who knows him well and then say something great about Tim. It can be as simple as you really like Tim, to something more specific, like the way he works or leads. It could refer to a project he's working on and what a good job he's doing. It could be a general comment about how well liked or respected he is around the office.

My favourite way to talk behind somebody's back like this is to repeat a conversation that probably happened with me and a colleague.

- *Do you know, I was talking to someone about who we most admire in this company and Tim's name came up.*
- *I was chatting to a colleague just last week about the best rainmakers/leaders/project managers/sales people in this department and Tim was the one person we both thought of.*

It's an indirect but effective way to get a message back to someone influential that makes them think well of you. Which does your prominence no harm whatsoever.

40. Think up ideas and projects

Few things give you visibility like a new idea. Ideas and projects kick-start conversations. What new initiatives can you dream up that would add value to the company? Anything new is a great excuse to get people's opinions and comments. It's a reason to invite people to talk. It's another excuse to create engagement. Be an initiator, an entrepreneur, an inventor. It increases your visibility.

41. Celebrate your wins

When you do something good, share it. Celebrate it. Too often we play down our wins. We move quickly onto the next thing. Whether it's a tweet, a Facebook post, a LinkedIn update or a mention to a few good friends, make sure you get it out there. When people ask you how you're doing (which they always do) say 'Great. I've just …

- *... finished this huge project!'*
- *... nailed this tricky problem!'*
- *... made this great content!'*
- *... written my first blog!'*
- *... got myself set up on Twitter!'*
- *... won this new client!'*
- *... started this new role!'*

There are a hundred things you could celebrate today if you choose to. Whether it's business or personal, work or social, find a way to rejoice in your success. It creates conversations, shares your achievements and makes people talk about you.

Summary: Profile toolbox

The strategy for survival is visibility. It was Woody Allen who said that '50% of success is simply showing up!' You must 'get out there' and raise your profile if you want to build your reputation. Being anonymous will not serve your purpose. You've got to get in the game. You've got to see and be seen. Notice and be noticed. Get on people's radars. Become a presence at key events.

You've just had 41 amazing ways to enhance your profile and boost your visibility. You don't need all of them. Just a handful that will work for you. You're good, but if you're a nobody then you're just ordinary. Putting yourself forward may be awkward for you. Particularly if you're something of an introvert. But it's the only way to prevent your anonymity.

This stuff is like a muscle. You can train it. You can hone it. You can get better. Things like networking are not easy for a lot of people, but it's all coachable. By pushing yourself, trying new things and being courageous, you're going to be the one with the exceptional reputation and amazing connections.

Chapter 7

Your Positioning Toolbox: Authority

'The way to gain good reputation is to endeavour to be what you desire to appear.'

– Socrates

Content – contribution – authority

This Reputation Toolbox gives you 35 things you can do to position yourself favourably in front of your target audience. It's all about your content and contribution. If you need to, read the Authority Blueprint again to embed these principles of expert status.

Positioning your brilliance means telling people who you are, what you do and how you do it. You want to differentiate yourself and build credibility. It's no good being everywhere but having nothing to say. This is about messaging. Thought leadership. Content creation. Sharing your thoughts and your ideas. Positioning you as a player in your space.

The overall message here is **become an authority**. That's above and beyond doing a great job. Being good is a given. This is extra. It's what sets you apart from mere technical and functional competence. Without the right positioning, you can have all the profile in the world but you'd be saying nothing. This toolbox in five words: Create content. Become an authority.

1. Turn your weaknesses into strengths

This is a self-talk strategy to keep you confident. It recalibrates your personal dialogue and begins to correct what others might be saying about you. Look out for any words on the left side that you find yourself saying in your personal talk. Or you might consider whether anyone has ever used any of those words to describe you. Then replace them with the words on the right.

What you might say about yourself or what others might say about you	What you're going to replace it with, both in your own head and in their dialogue
Disorganized or Messy	Creative or Quirky
Shy or Quiet	Thoughtful or Reflective
Stubborn or Inflexible	Committed or Determined
Inconsistent or Flakey	Flexible or Open
Intense or Uptight	Single-Minded or Focused
Cold or Emotionless	Deep or Calm
Dull or Boring	Responsible or Dependable
Unrealistic or Impractical	Positive or Optimistic
Negative or Critical	Realistic or Practical
Intimidating or Arrogant	Assertive or Confident
Weak or Soft	Humble or Gracious
Indecisive or Hesitant	Patient or Contemplative
Impatient or Edgy	Passionate or Enthusiastic
Impetuous or Impulsive	Decisive or Quick-Thinking

Don't let anyone say negative things about you. If one person dislikes the fact that you work hard and long hours (perhaps they're jealous!) they may say you're 'sucking up' or making others look bad. Your reframe is that you're diligent and just wanting to do a good job. Remember: every weakness has a corresponding strength.

2. Become a thought leader

It's more than a buzzword or reputational ideal. Thought leadership is the systematic creation and positioning of useful content for a particular audience. You draw from your experience, your intelligence, your expertise. You give answers to questions that matter. You provide clarity in fog. And wisdom in folly.

There's a really useful guide to this stuff in the Reputation Vault. It's the Thought Leadership Manifesto. It's got great questions to ask yourself over becoming a thought leader, plus the kind of things thought leaders do. Might be worth a read.

3. Become an authority

Remember the different ways you can become an expert or stand-out authority from Chapter 5? Let's recap.

- **The Creators**. These people come up with new stuff. Or new ways of thinking about old stuff. They are thinkers and dreamers. They are inventors and makers. They initiate and originate. If you have a tendency to disrupt, you might choose the Creator route to establish your authority. The contribution of Creators is original and disturbing.
- **The Networkers**. These people are hubs and social magnets. They create value through connecting people to information, ideas and each other. They attract. They organize. They persuade. They convene. If you're a people person and want to become indispensable, this is your route. The contribution of Networkers is experiential and engaging.

- **The Reporters**. These people help everyone make sense of the world. They are knowledge organizers and content curators. They report. They research. They investigate. They become the authority because of their hunger for information and meaning. If you are naturally curious and a strong communicator, become a Reporter. The contribution of Reporters is expressive and meaningful.
- **The Genius**. These people have an exceptional natural capacity of intellect. Intelligence. Ingenuity. Mental giants. Their special gifts, flair and wizardry give them distinctive character and spirit. If you feel 'special' you can stand out. You're not quite a mutant or an abnorm, but you're out there in a beautiful way. The contribution of the Genius is brilliant and passionate.

Pick your lane, your best route to authority status. It's an incredibly powerful way to position yourself as the exceptional candidate, leader or expert in any given situation.

4. Write a manifesto

Remember the Tom Cruise movie 'Jerry McGuire'. 'Show me the money!' might jog your memory. Central to the movie was the Manifesto for a new way of servicing sports clients. Manifestos can be written on various topics. We've got at least 20 of them in the Reputation Vault.

Manifestos tell your stakeholders what you're made of. They offer a deeper insight into your philosophies and ideas. They are a really powerful way for you to stand out in a crowd.

5. Use your email signature

Everywhere your name appears, it's a chance to reinforce your personal brand. With the billions of emails flying around, your email signature (what you put at the bottom of each one) is a useful positioning tool.

Include as much info as you can. Any tag-lines, core messages and 'unique value propositions' remind people what you do really well. Perhaps add a testimonial or quote from a satisfied stakeholder. You could add a 'call to action' by asking people to check out a book or blog that you've written.

Make your website name and email address consistent. Don't waste a branding opportunity by just signing your name. You could also have different email signatures that you insert depending on your audience. It keeps your emails personal, relevant and professional.

6. Take control of conversations

If you find some conversations getting away from you, it's time to take charge. There are three main dynamics in a conversation: seniority, passion and expertise. Any one of these will give you the edge. Any two will give you ultimate control.

As an example, senior people usually talk more, challenge more, interrupt more and direct conversations more. They ask the questions and pick the topics of conversation. If you're not senior but you want to gain control of a conversation, maybe to communicate your ideas, you can nullify seniority with passion, enthusiasm and emotion.

Witness the impact of a moving speech, a tear-jerking song rendition or a zealous salesman. Couple this with some knowledge or expertise and you can soon take command of a situation. When positioning your authority and influencing power players, leverage your expertise with emotion and you'll hopefully gain more control in your conversations.

7. Articulate your points of difference

What are your PODs? When you talk about the same stuff your rivals talk about, you sound just like them. These are called Points of Parity (POPs) – the stuff you have in common with others. PODs give people a reason to switch or choose you.

Anything you can do that's unique or distinctive gives you a POD. If there are too many POPs or similarities, you're simply a 'me-too' proposition. You also can't be too differentiated or you'll be perceived as too radical, too 'out there' and possibly not covering the core needs for the target market.

If you have a POD, don't just mention it. Exaggerate it. Talk up the benefits of it and explain why it makes you the stand-out choice in any given situation. So your language should be *'yes I do that too, but I can also offer you this ... '.*

8. Articulate a distinct viewpoint

Try to sound and look a little bit different to your peers. It's a subtle yet effective way to stand out. You don't have to swim against the tide and be totally opposite. But coming at things a little off-centre can get you noticed.

Look for opportunities to question, challenge and pivot away from the mainstream. Your contribution will be noticed for being different, even if it's misunderstood or disagreed with. And if you communicate with confidence and vigour, you might just bring a few round to your way of thinking.

9. Leave out 'nothing words'

To communicate 'authority', you've got to sound right. What dilutes your impact are the many 'nothing words' that have crept into people's everyday language. Here's a list of the most common

- *Literally ...*
- *Obviously ...*
- *Basically ...*
- *I mean ...*
- *Probably ...*

- *Kinda (kind of) ...*
- *I think ...*
- *Erm ...*
- *Like ...*
- *Sort of ...*
- *You know ...*
- *You know what I mean ... ?*

All of these extra words drown out your key message. You don't write like that, so why speak like that? They add nothing. They take away attention from your main words.

Maybe you get lazy. Perhaps you're so scared of losing control of a conversation that you fill any pauses with nothing words to keep talking. Either way, it's not good for your positioning. Stop it.

10. Stop saying 'you're welcome!'

This seems an odd tactic for building your reputation, so let's explore. Often the best way to build your good name is to lock in value when you create it. In other words, if you do something great, don't play it down.

Here's how it works. When clients tell you you've done a terrific job, you'll probably reply – 'you're welcome' or 'it's nothing'. Worse, you tell them 'no problem'. When really it was a big deal, and you did put yourself out!

If you move heaven and earth for them, and tell them it was nothing, you do your reputation no good at all. Capitalize on these opportunities to let people know you've really gone out of your way for them. Don't say 'you're welcome' anymore. Instead, use something like 'I really appreciate you saying that – I wouldn't do that for everybody' or 'That's okay. I'm sure you'd do the same for me if you had the chance.'

11. Ask great questions

It's said you can tell more about a person by the questions they ask than the answers they give. You can show your brilliance or your ignorance with a question. That's why you need the right and the best questions.

They say wherever you want a conversation to go, the right question will take you there. The ability to ask insightful questions cuts across the credibility gap. That's the chasm created by senior people when they look down on young people.

If you find yourself being judged by those crusty, superficial, dark-suited men (yes it's mostly men!) then speak less, listen more and ask great questions. They'll soon start taking you seriously.

12. Develop power scripts

Craft and use great questions and also have strong answers ready for tough questions. The worst time to think of the best thing to say is as the words are coming out of your mouth. If a conversation has something at stake, you should prepare for it.

The best sales people, the best parents, the best leaders, the best managers – they all have certain scripts, questions and phrases that they use over and over again. They may not realize it, but they know deep down that these words get results. Perhaps you already have some killer phrases that work for you in particular situations.

Power scripts open doors and create opportunities. They diffuse situations and influence people for your benefit. They give you an unfair competitive advantage because you're ready with the right line at the right time.

Some people think scripts are too, well, scripted. But if there's a killer word, phrase or question that will unlock a particular opportunity for you at a particular time, then why bother making it up on the spot? Use what works.

The problem people have with scripts is that they sound like a script. So say them naturally, and nobody will ever know that you prepared it in advance. A power script is the right words said at the right time to deliver the right result, prepared in advance and delivered in a natural yet compelling way.

The right word said at the right time to the right person can open a world of opportunities. Here are some opportunities to use power scripts:

- Saying 'no' to people.
- Giving your elevator pitch (your answer to 'what do you do?').
- Objection handling in sales.
- Job interview questions and good answers.
- Dealing with difficult staff and colleagues.
- Crucial conversations with superiors.

There are so many critical situations that you can't afford to leave to chance. Your reputation could depend on it. If this topic really interests you, we've done you a Power Script Manifesto in the Reputation Vault. Check it out.

13. Speak in public

Any Q&A sessions, panels, discussion groups, conferences or association meetings you can speak at, do it. Speaking is fantastic for your profile because you can market yourself 'one to many' versus 'one to one' as in a networking scenario.

Speaking is also great for your credibility and authority because very few others actually want to do it. They admire you for being up there AND they admire you for what you're saying. Double positioning bonus. Speaking is good for many reasons. Do it more. Do it well. Someday people will actually pay you for doing it!

14. Focus your efforts

It's hard to be everything to everyone. You perhaps already know that the word 'focus' nicely equals 'Follow One Course Until Successful'. Where you apply your best thinking, your strongest pressure, your greatest effort is where you'll have the biggest impact.

Beware spreading yourself too thinly. You'll see later the power of niching. Any kind of focus prevents you from becoming a generalist. You want specialist status. That's what commands respect and authority. Have more discipline in saying 'no' to a few things. That way you can focus more.

Finally on focus. Beware your biggest enemy. *Distraction*. Stay on the Yellow Brick Road. Venturing off the path is only going to get you there slower, if at all.

15. Say 'no' to the good

This comes from a quote from leadership guru John Maxwell. *'Say no to the good so you can say yes to the great.'* Try saying 'yes' to ordinary tasks, ordinary people, ordinary opportunities. You'll soon be so busy and blinkered that you (a) won't even see the extraordinary stuff and (b) won't have the bandwidth to do anything about it if you do.

When you hang out with the wrong people, doing the wrong stuff, you get dragged down. Gossip. Distraction. Mediocrity. Poor health. None of this earns you career capital. Be strong. Say 'no' to some of the good stuff so you're ready and waiting for the great stuff.

16. Craft strong elevator pitches

The 'what do you do?' question will come up in 98% of conversations with a stranger. You need a good reply. This is your elevator speech or pitch – a short phrase that takes seconds to say but will get you noticed and remembered. If you know it's coming, get your pitch ready. A variety of answers for different audiences, situations and time lengths is vital for any respected networker and reputation builder.

When people ask you what you do, you've got one shot to make an impression. This may stay with them forever or they may forget about you in seconds. When people ask you what you do, they're actually asking you who you are and how you make a difference. Have a number of strong answers that you've created in advance for key situations and audiences.

The best pitches involve stories and examples of:

- what you've done that made a difference
- why you're better or different
- why clients, customers or employers choose you
- what you're currently working on
- your areas of speciality or expertise.

These are the most powerful pitches you can deliver because when you relate instances like this, people (a) remember them and (b) pass them onto others. That gives you great positioning and authority.

17. Work a niche

It's harder to be an authority in everything and for everyone. See if you can establish some kind of niche. There are many ways to niche. By what you do. By how you do it. By who you do it for. And by where you do it. Have a think about where you could narrow your focus to provide more meaningful content.

With no niche, you're a generalist. You really want to be a specialist. The narrower the niche, the smaller the audience. But the less the competition and the greater the 'pre-eminence'. Be aware of who's doing what around you. Look for the gaps. That's where you'll make your biggest mark.

18. Create a new category

In a crowded, predatory marketplace, you're looking for a small slice of attention. You're looking to stand out in some small but significant way. Differentiate or lose, right? If you can be the first to cater to a new market, or the first to create an alternative service, then you are suddenly in a category with no competitors. It may only be a case of adjusting or customizing your existing skills or approach rather than doing something entirely new.

Creating a 'category of one' is a clever reputation-building strategy because it positions you differently. It eliminates the crowd and rarefies the competitive atmosphere.

- So could you be the first, best, cheapest, latest, oldest, newest, fastest, closest, biggest, smallest or safest?
- Are you the most entrepreneurial, radical, convenient, innovative, experimental, strategic, thorough, global, positive, relationship-based, profit-centric, results-focused or customer-led?
- As well as the stuff your competitors do, are you also an author, thought leader, innovator, campaigner, speaker, coach, mentor, consultant, connector, philanthropist or problem-solver?

You've got to have some edge. Some hook. Something to set you apart. Only needs to be slight. Just enough. Enough to make people choose you, think of you, bring you into their mind, go for you instead of your competition. That's what creates an outstanding reputation.

19. Craft your back story

How did you come to be where you are? This is your back story. Your personal narrative. It's what gives you the credibility to step out and speak with authority. People will be interested in your story. Your highs and lows. Your milestones. Your struggles.

Your back story makes you human. People will relate to you and like you even more. You'll tell them your why – why you got into this game and why you love it so much. You'll show them why you know so much about your areas of expertise. You'll share your personal stories of breakthrough and your incredible ideas. You'll chart your course from zero to hero. Shallow to deep. And they'll love you for it.

20. Promote yourself elegantly

Sometimes called ethical bragging, when you can elegantly and subtly promote yourself, you underline your credentials for greatness. People like winners, so downplaying your achievements will hurt you.

Obviously you don't want to sound like an arrogant jerk or big-headed show off. There is a time and a place for blowing your own trumpet. When people ask you how things are going – that's a good opportunity to share what you've been working on and what you've achieved. Telling stories to illustrate how you came through is also a subtler way.

If this is a problem for you (and it tends to trouble women more than men) then we've done you a Self-Promotion Manifesto with lots of useful tips on ethical bragging and elegant personal marketing. Check it out.

21. Know what you're worth

Have you ever stopped to think about your hourly or daily rate? Not what you charge out to clients, but how much you get paid by your company. It's a good calculation, because it will tell you how much of an authority you are.

There are approximately 250 working days in a year. If you earned $4,000 per day, you would reach the million-dollar mark each year; $400 per day is $100K per year. Building your reputation and amassing career capital will eventually increase what you're worth and grow your daily rate. Get in the habit of charging premium because that will create an expectation that you'll work hard to position yourself for the reward.

22. Widen your horizons

Every time you bring fresh ideas and perspective back into your company, you add value. You create career capital. You provide valuable 'bring-back' for your network. This contribution hopefully gets noticed by your stake-holders.

So widen your horizons and look more outward to see what you can learn from what's happening out there. You could start by following a few external thought leaders, business figures or companies on Twitter or LinkedIn. You could be meeting up with a few people in different industries and asking 'what's new?'

Follow discussions, trends and statistics. Think about what's coming up on the horizon for your field, your profession, your industry. Comment on it. Write about it. This turns you into a thought leader.

23. Manage your online reputation

Back in the day, your hallway reputation was all that mattered. These days you've got a whole new world to take care of. Your online reputation is your 'Google-ability'. You need to harness the power of the internet because, if you're not findable on Google, you're pretty much 'career invisible'.

Where do you show up out there in the Internet of Things? Is there any bad or weak stuff out there? Can you push it down the Google pages with your good stuff so nobody sees it? We've done you a special Online Reputation Manifesto with the rules of managing your good name online. You'll also get lots of great tips for specifically harnessing and controlling the online space for maximum positive impact. Go to the Reputation Vault and download it now.

24. Adopt a noble cause

What's your big crusade? Your issue that you want to put right? Your burning passion? People are attracted to worthy causes and passionate ambassadors of those causes. You don't need to go all out by adopting a child in India, saving llamas in Tibet or halting corruption in the South American transport system.

Think what's wrong with your company or organization. Your firm. Your department or division. Your industry. Your profession. Your town or street. Your country. What habit, practice, procedure or policy needs changing? What document needs rewriting? What tradition needs abolishing or resurrecting?

Embracing an honourable and upright cause gains you respect, sympathy and attention. Your commitment and contribution to the fight is duly noted and gains you massive reputational points. Which is a nice bonus on top of the difference you're making to the world.

25. Play hard to get

Expensive, premium and rare things become more and more exclusive. The more difficult something is to attain, the more you value it. It's human nature. Of course, you want to be accessible and reliable. At the same time, sitting by the phone and picking it up after one ring shows you're not too unavailable.

Your authority status is underlined by you being hard to reach. By your full diary. By your list of commitments. You're in demand, remember. Positioning yourself as always 'in play' puts you in the middle of, rather than ahead of, the pack. Be a little more unattainable and your reputation might just go up a notch.

26. Decide MWR for each interaction

MWR is 'most wanted response'. People who know what they want are compelling to watch. They usually get it too. Consider carefully what you want from every conversation, encounter, phone call, meeting, blog post or presentation.

MWR is specific. So what do you actually want people to think, do, feel and say next? When you're clear on your objective, you can be much more purposeful in leading them there. This is power positioning. People who persuade, influence and get what they want are usually considered authorities.

27. Get media attention

If you've dipped into the Profile Toolbox, you'll see some great tips on getting into print media and on radio and television. This is great for profile but also great for disseminating your opinions, ideas and arguments.

When you've got something to say or a contribution to make, you've got to let the world know. The media is great for that. Don't be overwhelmed. We're not talking national TV or press just yet. You can start small and local.

Contact local radio and TV stations or newspapers that serve small markets. They're always looking for story ideas and angles. Reach out to your network to see if any have media connections. As you become well known, you'll be more in demand for the higher profile opportunities.

28. Partner with VIPs

One of the most impactful ways to position yourself is to associate with powerful people. It's called the 'Oprah Effect'. Just standing close to 'celebrities' suggests you're endorsed, vouched for and on par with them. You become their peer rather than their fan, at least in the eyes of others.

People like winners. And when you associate with winners, a little of the magic rubs off. Be courageous and reach out to the VIPs.[1]

29. Borrow the credibility of others

You know the power of getting around the right people. This is great for profile and also for authority status. It's said that authority is like glitter. Those who come in contact with it can't help but leave with a little on their sleeve.

You gain reverence and status by coupling with the leaders and influences in your world. You borrow some of their huge credibility until you have enough of your own. People think if you're hanging around with them, you must be just as good.

There are many ways to give back value to these demi-gods. There's a special Give Back Manifesto in the Reputation Vault with lots of tips on how to make influencers want to help you. If you can create a 'value for value' exchange, you're got almost instant authority.

30. Gather and use testimonials

Most people claim to be great at what they do. Yet it becomes hard to choose between truth and lies. Telling the world how good you are is one thing. Getting others to do that for you is quite another. And much more powerful.

What people say about you is ten times more effective than what you say about yourself. This third party endorsement or recommendation holds so much more power than your own claims. It gives you far more credibility. Others will always sell you better than you sell yourself.

---

[1]Remember there's a great Give-Back Manifesto in the Reputation Vault with lots of suggestions to encourage powerful people to help you in return.

There are plenty of people ready to lavish praise on you. But they won't do it unsolicited. Which means you need to ask. There are three ways you could do this:

1. **Write to them**. Send an email or LinkedIn message to a few key stakeholders or good friends. Ask them for an endorsement or recommendation of your expertise. You can even offer to do the same for them – a mutual back scratch.
2. **Talk to them**. Ask a few close people face to face if they'd consider doing you a testimonial about your work sometime. Then sit back and wait for it to come in. If they don't know what to say, you could always give them a few ideas or key phrases they may adapt. Best to stop short of actually writing it for them!
3. **Wait for openings**. Look for *moments of truth* when you can ask on the spot. For instance, when people thank you or say what a good job you've done, ask if they would mind putting it in writing. Better still, ask them to post it on LinkedIn so the world can see.

Letting other people do your talking is social proof and a very powerful expert trigger. Testimonials are clear evidence for your supremacy. Instead of waiting for it to fall into your lap, take an active role and gather as many honest and compelling testimonials as you can.

31. Create content

Beyond doing a stand-out job, content is your primary contribution to your authority status. Creating content simply means writing blogs, doing videos, creating podcasts and similar stuff to get your thinking out there. This could be online or in print or in person. Two quick tips[2] on doing this right so it cuts through the noise and is valued by your audience:

1. **Keep it evergreen**. In other words, don't date it in a way that people reading down the road think it's irrelevant.

---

[2]You can also find a Content Manifesto in the Reputation Vault, with lots more tips like this to help you create and market your ideas and your fabulous content.

2. **Repurpose it**. One blog post can be carved up lots of different ways to leverage your efforts. This also gets the word out across different platforms. So it could be turned into infographics, tweets and recordings.

32. Create videos

More and more online searches are bringing up videos. The biggest search engine in the world (Google) owns the biggest video site in the world (YouTube). YouTube has over 3 billion searches every month, with hundreds of hours of footage uploaded every minute.

Everyone loves video. The vast majority of people online watch videos every day. According to Forbes, 75% of executives watch work-related videos on business websites at least once a week; 50% watch business-related videos on YouTube; and 65% of these people visit the mentioned website after watching a video. So if you can use videos to enthuse executives and grab attention, you're positioning yourself in front of a hungry crowd.

33. Go mobile

More than 50% of internet traffic is now viewed on a mobile device. What are you doing to access that audience? You've got to be present on all mediums. Getting good with the various mobile apps and technologies is vital for your continued relevance.

How good are you at creating content and keeping in touch 'on the go?' It's the future, particularly with the tech-savvy digital-native millennials coming through the employment pipeline. These people will rule the world soon. So let's serve them as best we can by getting on their wavelength and communicating to them using all the mobile tools at our disposal.

34. Create a COC

COC stand for conference, organization or community. People who create big things like this or make events happen are given huge authority status. This is contribution on a large scale. Putting on an awards evening, holding an expert summit, hosting a Q&A with a major industry figure. All of these big deals get you on the map.

Is there an organization or movement waiting to be started? What about a community you could get going? Where's the gap? The hungry crowd? What's missing out there that you could supply? Creating some kind of COC could cement your legacy and your reputation for years to come.

35. Own your reputation

Never be scared of calling yourself an expert or an authority. Whether you feel like it or not, you've got to own your space. You probably know more than 95% of people in your particular and specific area. So claim it.

Of course, even if you've put in years of delivering, learning, creating and contributing, you may still be reluctant to claim 'stand-out' status. Perhaps you're fearful of getting found out or letting people down. Maybe the pressure to deliver on bigger and bigger stages with more and more at stake scares you.

You'll grow into it. It may seem frightening now, but you'll get more and more comfortable in your brilliance. As you develop more career capital and a stronger reputation, you'll learn that people's perceptions are the reality. If they think you're the expert, then you are. So live with it!

Summary: Positioning board toolbox

The positioning part of building a reputation says that building a network and raising your profile are important. But having something to say completes the piece, educating others on your vision, insight and expertise. Beyond your initial circles of influence, you need some kind of platform for your thought leadership and achievements.

Your thoughts, ideas, knowledge, presence and other tradeable career commodities need putting out there. People need to know how good you are. This is the realm of authority status and producing content. There is a hungry audience just waiting for you. An audience that's just your size and wants just your take on just your kind of interests. It might not be a huge audience, but everyone starts small.

Even if nobody reads your stuff when you create it, you're building online credibility and thought leadership which adds to your overall reputation. This will get you noticed through purposeful personal marketing across a number of channels.

Positioning yourself is not just through your content. It's in the way you talk about yourself. The way you come over in conversations, language, interactions. You've got to walk the walk and talk the talk. Only then will people start to believe that you truly are the real thing. Which is what gets you hired, promoted and given the opportunities to do the work you love on your terms. #careercapital

Chapter 8

Your Personal Board Toolbox: Network

'Associate yourself with people of good quality, for it is better to be alone than in bad company.'

– Booker T. Washington

Network – advocates – leverage

This Reputation Toolbox features advanced networking strategies to leverage your best connections. A network in and of itself is just a bunch of names. When you can summon the help of superheroes and advocates that have your back, you're cooking. We call this a Personal Board of Advisors (PBA).

Everyone says that the higher up you go, the lonelier it is. Every promotion creates a wedge between the friends and colleagues you used to have but now can't play 'mates' with any more. There are fewer people available and equipped to help you make key decisions and weather tough storms. This is made worse if you've neglected your networking.

You must intentionally get around the right people. You need advocates and champions. You need door openers and specialists. You need to be the leverage that comes from the networks and influence of others.

You know by now the importance of defining and strategically building your ideal network. When you can source and nurture powerful connections, you open up a world of possibilities.

This Reputation Toolbox is about refining your connections and leveraging them to further your goals. Specifically, it's about carefully selecting and 'promoting' the best people to be on your PBA.

Everything in here is about high-level networking. And exploiting that network in a 'value for value' exchange that benefits all parties. Especially you. Pick as many of these as you can handle to appoint your inner circle or PBA. And work hard to get the king or queen of the pack – that all important sponsor.

Remember: these will probably arise from relationships you already have. So in calibrating your network, ask yourself who could step up to play a more influential role in your life, and how you might motivate them to do so.

1. Assess the value of each connection

People say networking is about giving, supporting and helping others. I get that. Try always to think what you can do for people rather than what they can do for you. But you're strategically building a network here. That means assessing the value of each connection.

When evaluating the legitimacy and usefulness of somebody coming into your network, think selfishly about these five questions:

1. **Their usefulness**. How useful might they be to you in adding to your career capital? What experience skills, knowledge or attributes do they bring to your life?
2. **Their credibility**. Can you name drop them for kudos and credibility? How good is it for your reputation and good name to be associated with them? Can you leverage them for introductions and endorsements?
3. **Their network**. What doors might they open for you? Who might they know that could help you?
4. **Their benevolence**. How willing might they be to help you? Can you call upon them for advocacy or sponsorship? Can you lean on them for help and advice?
5. **Their challenges**. If I bring this person into my PBA, what might I offer them in return? What challenges, pain or projects do they have that I can help them with?

If you get favourable answers to these questions, you can recruit valued partners in the Career Game.

2. Tap into the hidden job market

It's claimed that 90% of jobs are never advertised. They come through the hidden job market. 'It's not what you know but who you know' and all that. It's called the hidden job market. Your next opportunity will probably come through someone you know.

Whether it's a strong or a weak tie, the ability of your network to open doors, 'put in a word' or flag up possible openings is not to be underestimated. If a prime position turns up in a newspaper or online job board, it's probably already been filled. Here are five great tips for tapping more intentionally into this world of hidden opportunities.

1. **Don't be a secret**. Use the script: '*If you come across/if you hear anything about [state what you're looking for or what you want an opportunity to do] then don't keep me a secret.*'
2. **Reach into their network**. Use the script: '*Do you know anyone who needs or is looking for [whatever you can do or want to do]?*'
3. **Use possibility words**. This takes the pressure off what you're asking. Examples – *could you possibly … might you be able to … do you know anyone that perhaps … if you maybe hear about …*
4. **Use examples**. This is great to illustrate what you want. So say things like: '*I heard of an opening for X last week. If you come across anything similar …*' Or '*I went for this role recently. It's not quite right for me but if you hear of a similar opening …*'
5. **Ask them first**. If you ask people what they're looking for or how you can help them, it's likely they'll reciprocate. This gives you the opportunity to fill them in on what's a good fit for you.

Be intentional in the way you put yourself out there. Every conversation, cup of coffee, beer, corridor chat or one-to-one meeting is an opportunity for you to subtly share your shopping list. If you can't or won't do this, the hidden job market stays hidden.

3. Let people in the loop

Keep people informed of your desires and opportunities. Let them know the kind of thing you're looking for. Keep them in the loop with interviews and expressions of interest.

Your network can't feed you if they don't know what you're hungry for. In the absence of a steer from you on the kind of opportunities that appeal, they'll offer you everything or nothing. It's your responsibility to educate and update.

Some of this will be online and via social media, which will reach your wider network. Other communication will be corridor conversations. Face-to-face stuff. Particularly if you can get close to people.

Let people in on what you're currently working on and what's exciting you. That's often the best indicator of what else they can put your way. By sowing seeds of what you need and what you're looking for, you're more likely to make it happen.

Set up meetings, catch ups and conversations to check in with people. Ask how they're doing and they'll do the same for you. Every opportunity you get to answer the 'how's it going?' or 'how are you doing?' questions is another chance to keep people in the loop.

Share what you're chasing, what you're hoping for, what you're working towards. If people don't know what you're doing and where you're going, they can't help you. Even if they want to.

4. Understand why people get hired, chosen and promoted

This is the smart way to leverage your network and your career capital. If you're going to be in the right place at the right time for your network to put you forward for something, pay attention to hiring dynamics. You can get hired, chosen or promoted for any of the following reasons:

1. **You hit plan or exceed your targets**. This could be for getting stuff done or bringing in new business.
2. **You exhibit strong functional skills**. Thus your technical performance in role is better than average.
3. **You get lucky**. You're the right person at the right time. Your face fits and somebody up there likes you.
4. **You serve your time**. Just by sticking around, you become the 'last man standing'.
5. **You're good with people**. You show some talent in getting on with others.

6. **Nobody else volunteers**. It's a poisoned chalice. Nobody wants the job and everyone takes a step back.

Once you get attuned to the subtleties of hiring and firing, you can read situations to your advantage. Of course, some of this will be pure luck. You just happen to be in the right place at the right time. But you can create your luck by observing the office politics, discerning the trends and reading the signs. Remember you're in a game. Know it and play it. That's what the Career Pros do.

5. Turn things down

Sometimes a well-meaning recommendation or offer from your network results in a 'wrong un'. It's not quite the right fit. It's not really what you're looking for. Yet you don't want to upset the giver as they're influential and sincere. What do you do?

Bottom line, you've got to 'fess up'. Be honest. Sometimes you're not ready to step up. You may need a step out – sideways or into a different sphere. If you turn something down, give a good reason. Perhaps you haven't yet developed enough leadership skills or technical know-how.

Perhaps you haven't yet assembled the right kind of connections that will equip you for such a role. Maybe it's the case that you just don't fancy it. Be gracious, be thankful and be complimentary. Be truthful and be humble. Maintain all links, keep all doors open and all bridges intact.

Take the opportunity to re-iterate what would be a good opportunity for you. *'This wasn't right for me because _____ but if you hear of anything in _____ then I'd love to be in the mix.'*

Sometimes what you say 'no' to can define you better than what you say 'yes' to. That's why niches work in marketing. That's why women love marriage proposals. It's not that the man is saying 'yes' to them.

It's that he's saying 'no' to every other woman on the planet. Forever. Hope I've not scared any of you fellas with that! Find better ways to say 'no'.[1]

6. Say 'thank you' more and better

Thank you means something in any language. Showing appreciation to your network, and particularly your PBA, is a smart thing to do. Studies show that saying thank you means people remember you more, buy what you're selling and talk about you more.

Of course, you already say 'thank you', right? So how do you stand out with that? It's how you do it. A good habit to get into is sending thank you cards. A handwritten thank you card goes even further. They don't take long to write and they pleasantly surprise because almost nobody does them.

Think about it. You'll stand out massively if only because you've taken the time. Here are three extra tips about sending thank you cards to your stakeholders.

1. **Be specific with your thanks**. Don't just thank them. Mention a specific gesture, task, comment or time.
2. **Mention outcomes**. *'Thank you for doing X. It meant that I could do Y.'* What's the endgame, the outcome of their action? What did their kind act enable you to do or be free of? Talk about their impact, not just their action.
3. **Be emotional**. Mention how it made you feel. 'I was amazed' and 'I was thrilled' show your deep gratitude and even excitement at what they've done for you.

---

[1]There's a Saying No Manifesto in the Reputation Vault to help you with this. It contains lots of tips and scripts for turning stuff down but keeping lines open. Well worth a read, else you're going to land yourself in a world of pain by saying 'yes' to the wrong thing.

4. **Send it in the post**. Sometimes you'll deliver it by hand. If that's geographically tough, see if you can get their home or work address. People don't get nice cards in the mail anymore.
5. **Use online sites**. There are lots of online sites which will produce and personalize a thank you card, and send it where it needs to go.
6. **Be impromptu**. Buy a pack of thank you cards and carry them around with you. Even after a quick meeting, you can write one, stick a stamp on it and pop it in a mailbox back to where you've just been. They get it the next day and wow!

Of course, if you can't send a thank you card, use social media and emails. While not as good as cards, it's still better than saying it face to face or on the phone. Because it's in black and white. It's permanent. Say 'thank you' more and better. Make it a habit and watch your reputation gently rise.

7. Know what help you want

You've counted conversations. Now you've got to make them count. To use all that power, influence and ability to make things happen, you must know what you want. Most people can tell you what they don't want in life. *I don't want to be poor. I don't want to live there. I don't want to do that job.* But they can't articulate well what they do want.

To help you decide what you want from your network, let's dip into some brilliant research by Cathleen McGrath and Deone Zell in the MIT Sloan Management Review. Their paper 'Profiles of Trust: Who to Turn to and for What' reveals how top leaders and managers think strategically about what type of advice to seek from what type of person.

They studied the support networks of 50 senior executives (vice presidents, directors, general managers) who were part of a senior leadership development programme at a Fortune 50 firm. They found that people reached out for four types of support:

1. **Raw information**. Facts and figures. Data. Dates. Budgets. Trends. Spreadsheets. Targets. If you know where to look and who to ask, this is all easy to get. Largely thanks to technology.
2. **Actionable advice**. Opinion. Recommendations. Suggestions. Comment. Opportunities. All aimed at accomplishing something or making decisions. This kind of support is a bigger ask because more is at stake. The numbers never lie but my interpretation could be wrong. It requires wisdom, experience and confidence.
3. **Strategic or political help**. You want power and influence. Yet people are complicated. Organizations are complex. You need 'high stakes' support from smart people with strong emotional intelligence.
4. **Emotional support**. Sensitivity. Empathy. Familiarity. Complexity. This entails someone wanting help in working through difficult issues. You lean on people with compassion and integrity.

You can start to see what kind of people you would go to for what kind of support. You analyse your networking requirements in terms of the kind of support you need to achieve your career goals. Wrongly matching your needs to your support might cost you.

8. Rank the importance of your stakeholders

Every life is a life. All are created equal. Sure. But some are more equal than others. Which means you must nurture them differently, treat them differently and use them differently.

If you've identified your key players, you've got to decide which are the most important. A useful approach here is using a matrix or spreadsheet. Assess the value of each person on the following criteria. You could give them a ranking out of 5, with a high score indicating significant influence and low being fairly inconsequential.

1. Quality of their network (access to key decision makers).
2. Size of their network (following, fans, list).
3. Access to media or social media channels.

4. Possession of key knowledge or specialist skills.
5. Access to key knowledge or specialist skills.
6. Ability to influence the right people.
7. Quality of their personal reputation.
8. Interest in you and your world.
9. Relevant insight and experience.

You may have other criteria you'd want to add. It's your world, your job, your life. What's important to you in identifying those people who can help you in your quest?

9. Keep your stakeholders sweet

Stakeholders are people with a stake in your performance. What you do and how you do it matters to them. You can make them look good or bad. You can help or hinder them. Their fate is tied up in yours, for better or worse. It's good to know who these people are, what they want and what you need to do to keep them 'on side'.

Your reputational stakeholders are the people for whom your career capital, your success and your good name means something. It's obvious that your boss, supervisor or line manager is a stakeholder. They've invested in you. They hopefully care about you doing well, because they benefit by your positive contribution. It makes them look good.

Others will be colleagues and team members. Business partners, investors and shareholders. Possibly family members and life partners. If you're outward facing, then include customers, clients, suppliers and providers. They're all different. Different agendas, different personalities and different expectations. You should make it your business to find out what these are for each one.

If your reputation with these is weak or damaged, it's harder to move on and up. Like a weight around your neck, you'll be dragged back or held back. These people will write your references, testimonials and recommendations. These people will talk about you behind your back. Keep them sweet.

10. Recognize the saboteurs

They say keep your friends close and your enemies closer. The higher up you go, the more you'll get shot at. The further out you go as a change agent, entrepreneur or innovator, the more some people can resent you. That's why it's said you can always tell who the pioneers are because they have arrows in their back and are lying face down in the dirt.

When you do well or induce favour, some people suffer. It shouldn't be that way, but some jobs, professions and industries are 'winner takes all' environments. That means your success comes at the expense of others. It's not your fault but you do have to deal with it.

Saboteurs come in all shapes and sizes, with a range of different weapons. They blame you for their predicament. If it weren't for you, they'd have X or be able to do Y. They'll damage your reputation at worst and slow down your progress at best.

Recognize the saboteurs. From a few comments behind your back to more systematic undermining of your position, their tactics are cunning. So as you think of who might have the influence to affect your career, reflect on who could bring you down, hold you back or sully your good name.

For any negative stakeholders, you've got three choices. Ignore their impact, gain their support or manage their opposition. Whatever you do, you're in a much better position when you know who they are, what they're doing and why.

11. Ask for the help and advice you need

A network you can *lean on* and *draw from* is all-powerful. It's no good having a network and not using it. That's like having a banquet and not eating anything. You've worked hard to build all of that relationship capital. You know what kind of help you need. Now you just have to leverage it. That means exploiting it for maximum advantage.

That's why your network is primed. You've been investing in relationships and raising your profile. You've identified what you need your network to do for you. Once you know what help and advice you want, there are four ways to get it.

1. **Wait for it**. This is the polite way. The timid way. All good things come to those who wait, right? Maybe, you can't afford to play a reactive game, waiting for scraps to drop from the top tables of top influencers. Not a recommended strategy unless you're just killing time. Surely you'd rather get there in three years than seven?

2. **Ask for it**. This is the courageous way. You approach people and ask for the help and support you need. You get good people around you that you can ask for help and favour. An inner circle. A personal board. A mastermind group. If you're wondering why they should help you, we've got that covered and we'll come to it. For now, you just need to ask confidently and be worth it.

3. **Trade it**. Find some 'value for value' exchange and make a trade. Whether you do a contra deal, a barter, a *quid pro quo* or a 'you help me now and I'll help you later', any win–win approach can get you what you need.

4. **Take it**. This is a more aggressive approach which needs hustle and opportunism. Some people won't or can't give you what you need. Sometimes you just have to take it. You step up. You volunteer. You put yourself in the frame. You make things happen. You create your own luck.

Leverage your network. Extract the help and advice you need. Otherwise it's just a bunch of names.

12. Decide who you trust

As a leader or rising star, you need a support network you can trust. It improves your decision making, counters the pressures on you and increases your confidence to perform. It also protects your reputation as you make yourself more vulnerable. Reaching out for help and support might make folks think you're weak. They might take advantage.

You've got to choose carefully and create mutually strong exchanges. Trust is the currency of relationships. Trust means being vulnerable with people and letting your guard down. It involves appearing weak. Sure, you want to appear strong and capable. But that independence and proficiency often inhibits candid feedback.

Your judgement is critical when it comes to deciding who you trust for advice and support. Three factors tend to come into play:

1. **Ability and competence**. The skill, knowledge or experience someone has in a particular area. You might not lean on them in other areas where they are weak. Nobody can be good at everything.
2. **Compassion and empathy**. The intentions or motives of others and how they can relate to your situation. Do they have your best interests at heart?
3. **Integrity and character**. You will defer to people who are strong morally and share your values on what's important. You trust them to do and say the right thing, even at their own personal cost.

When you trust your network and they trust you, things get done faster. Barriers and suspicion are low. Motives are transparent. Cooperation is high. Collaboration is rampant. But trust takes time and discernment.[2]

---

[2]You'll find a special Trust Manifesto waiting for you in the Reputation Vault. If trust is a currency of relationships, you need to exploit its power in your plan for global domination.

13. Influence powerful people to help you

It's easy to say 'get around great people and you'll be okay' but you see the problem, right? It's another trade. Why should people help you and be there for you? Why should they lend their good name to yours to boost your career capital and employability? What's in it for them?

Influential, powerful people are often busy, important people. Unless your timing is exquisite and you tap up the right 'demi-god' then your pleas for aid may fall on deaf ears. These people rarely have either the time or the inclination to go out of their way and help you. Unless you can make it worth their while.

You may just get a break. Luck plays its part, for sure.[3] But it's not a smart, proactive and strategic way to gain career capital. Apart from anything else, it's just too darn reactive and unpredictable.

So what's the alternative? You must come up with ways to give back. If you want people to help you, you've got to earn it. You must be worth it to your connections. Valuable to the people you need. How do you do that? It's called a 'value for value' exchange.

Most people assume there is nothing you could possibly offer heavy hitters and powerful influencers. But that's not usually true. Everyone has problems and pain. Projects and plans. Everyone needs support, encouragement and endorsement. Nobody makes it alone.

Everyone needs something. These VIPs maybe won't tell you what they need. They might not even know. So if you want their help, sponsorship, connections or insight, you've got to earn it. That means finding out what people need so you can create a 'value for value' exchange.

---

[3] You'll find a special Luck Manifesto in the Reputation Vault to help you harness the power of serendipity in your domination of the universe.

When you give something of value and get something of value, everybody is happy. Knowing what you want from them is important. Knowing what you can offer in return is even more so. It's your job to either invent or discover the keys that will unlock the help of your desired network. That means do your homework. Due diligence. Find out. Even ask them.

Consider where they are in their careers. The transitions they are going through. There must be ways to give back and offer help that aren't easily available to them. Think hard. Be inventive. Come up with as many strategies as you can to create a solid 'value for value' exchange.[4]

14. Use the power of networking contra deals

One very effective way to source the skills and expertise you need is with contra deals. These are barters of goods and services without any exchange of money. Soft dollar deals. Favour for favour. You swap the stuff you're good at with the stuff someone else is good at. You shake hands on it and pledge to help each other.

They work because a lot of the time you're boot-strapping. You don't always have the money to invest in executive coaching, high-level mentoring or specialist skills. What you can't or won't pay for, you can still find and access with a contra deal.

You can 'contra' for help in all kinds of areas. Writing. Presenting. Phone technique. Networking. Techie stuff. Languages. Spreadsheets. Negotiating. Sales. PR. Social media. I've contra'd my skills in coaching in return for someone to teach me how to draw cartoons, prep me in a new language for an overseas trip, video editing and photography.

---

[4] You'll find a special Give-Back Manifesto in the Reputation Vault. It's crammed with brilliant stuff on the power of reciprocation (giving first) and how to use it to engage demi-gods. You'll also get 26 great ways to create value for these VIPs. Start utilizing some of these tactics to make their decision to help you an easy one that they are more than happy with.

This peer mentoring or peer coaching set up is becoming more and more popular. You want to help people anyway. It's in your nature. And guess what? They want to help you too. A contra deal just legitimatizes the arrangement.

If you're networking strategically and going wide, then you'll come across all kinds of people will all kinds of skills. They'll also have all kinds of needs and agendas. Some you'll be able to help with stuff they need. And that's when the magic happens.[5]

15. Create a solid contact strategy

You realize that building a potent network is all well and good, but how do you manage such a thing? This Reputation Toolbox has given you many ways to build and leverage your relationships. But managing a large network and getting it to a point of trust and credibility where it will help you is not easy.

A good contact strategy helps. It's best practice to segment your contacts into buckets, lists or labels. When you keep certain people in certain networks, you have a chance to manage that relationship. Our strongest relationships are characterized by high trust. High familiarity. These may include your PBA, top customers and clients, friends and family. You'll contact these pretty regularly. And get contact back.

A simple approach to do this is an ABCD classification. Your favourites, tier 1 or A-list close contacts should be very accessible. In networking terms these are called strong ties. Weekly or monthly contact is a minimum.

The B's are the secondary tier that you're nurturing. Contact frequency might be quarterly. The C's are a tertiary tier and might be contacted once

---

[5] There's a Contra Deal Manifesto waiting for you in the Reputation Vault if you want to know more.

or twice a year. The D's are for dumping, or at most playing reactively. That means you don't reach out to them – they have to come to you.

Then you'll have a lower tier or wider circle that you'll contact less regularly. These are weaker ties. You have a relationship with them and through others, but it's a little more reactive.

The best networkers, relationship builders and Career Pros recognize the value of all people but treat everyone differently. This benefits them as well as you. Of course, there is an even better way to maintain lots of high quality relationships …

16. Leverage technology to manage big networks

Realistically, how do you keep huge numbers of people happy, primed and informed? It is possible, although Dunbar's number says no. Dunbar's number describes the maximum number of people with whom you can maintain a meaningful relationship. These are relationships in which an individual knows who each person is and how each person relates to every other person.

Dunbar came across this number via Bill Gore, inventor of Gore-Tex fabrics. Gore found that his factories with more than 150 people were less likely to work effectively together as a team. Dunbar found similar results in Native American tribes, military units and Amish communities.

Strange, then, that your mobile phone has many more names than that. The average Facebook user has around 400 friends. LinkedIn users average 500 connections. I myself have 17,000. And we all seem to manage well enough. How come?

The secret is in getting organized. Not every contact has to be a handshake, a letter in the mail, a Christmas card or a phone call. There are a thousand ways to create a meaningful touch point that don't involve physical contact or excessive effort. You just have to be disciplined in how you do it.

You can try doing this with an old-fashioned Rolodex or filing system. You can get more sophisticated with spreadsheets and calendar reminders. But you know the smart way is to use the software and technology and social media platforms at your disposal.

The abundance of cool tools, apps and social networks gives you a chance. Social media is obviously a huge weapon for you. There are many CRM (contact relationship management) apps and tools to help you do this. Leverage technology to manage big networks and thus your reputation. That's how the Career Pros do it.

17. Prune your contacts continually

Remember: your network is who you know. Your reputation is who knows you. Of course, at some point you'll need to lose a few people. You can't manage millions. You need a smart way to evaluate who to keep and who to ditch.[6] This means some pruning.

In the 2004 film *The Girl Next Door* appears the phrase *'the juice is worth the squeeze'*. And the fact is, some people and relationships are simply not worth the effort you put into them. You love them, you invest in them, you forgive them, you show them grace and you help them. But they don't help you and they don't help themselves. The juice ain't worth the squeeze! Those are the people you've got to lose if you're going to rise to the top of your field.

Thus, one of the first steps in building a world-class network that will add serious clout to your career capital is to calibrate your existing network. That's going to mean getting rid of some people.

---

[6] You'll find a Contact Manifesto in the Reputation Vault. It explains more about strong and weak ties and gives you lots of clever ways to stay in meaningful contact with large numbers of people.

Sure, with lots of online platforms, cool apps and smart technology, you can manage bigger and bigger networks. You can keep these people hanging around. But the quality of your connections is often a better measure of your worth in the career market.

Colin Powell said, '*The less you associate with some people, the more your life will improve. Any time you tolerate mediocrity in others, it increases your mediocrity. An important attribute in successful people is their impatience with negative thinking and negative acting people.*'

Joel Osteen said that you cannot expect to hang out with negative people and have a positive life. Calibrating your network involves a critical evaluation of who is adding value to your career capital.

- **Who could be useful to me?** Now or in the future?
- **Who am I investing the most time in right now?** Is it worth it?

Losing some people gives you the head space and physical space to welcome others. You might just let them 'drift out to sea' by subtly not calling them back or returning emails. You might admit one to one that 'it's best you take a break' or go your separate ways. You may take a public stand and announce to the world that it's over. However you make the break, it's a healthy and wise thing to do.

Your career, your reputation, your peace of mind is at stake. To build, maintain and leverage a powerful network of all the right people, you've got to lose the wrong ones. So keep asking '*is the juice worth the squeeze?*'

18. Build higher level connections

Your game plan for building an outstanding reputation isn't 'make a lot of noise and throw it in all directions'. It's carefully crafted networking, purposefully forged alliances and diligently gathered career capital. It's dedicated personal marketing in the right direction at the right people.

Who notices you matters. You should work hard to (a) identify the people who need to know who you are for your own sake and (b) get on the radars of those people.

So, as well as your everyday stakeholders mentioned above, can you network at a higher, aspirational level? Who else might have some say in your success or otherwise? Here are seven questions which could help you identify the right people to keep close and make you look good:

1. **Power**. Who has the power and influence to affect your projects and plans?
2. **Interest**. Who might have an interest in you being successful?
3. **Influence**. Who might have the influence to affect your career?
4. **Access**. Who has access to resources, skills and connections that can make things easier for you?
5. **Opinion**. Whose opinion of you could make or break your career options?
6. **Benefit**. Who would benefit from knowing you?
7. **Solutions**. Who has problems that you could easily, innovatively or eventually solve?

Your list should show decision makers, employers and hirers. Influencers, VIPs and demi-gods of your industry. Movers, power players and corporate legends. Board-level executives. High-profile alumni. Directors, partners and CXOs and shakers in your company. Mentors and sponsors. Advisors and specialists.

Reach out to these people and build higher level connections. You will eventually recruit some of these onto your PBA, so find them and invest in them now. Then when you make the ask, you're likely to generate a more favourable response.

19. Recruit a sponsor

If you can only have one person to help you, there is a stand-out choice. They're called Sponsors. This is networking on steroids. Sylvia Ann

Hewlett, author of *Forget a Mentor, Find a Sponsor* explains how sponsors do so much more than mentors.

> *'If mentors help define the dream, ~~sponsors are the dream-enablers. Sponsors deliver.~~ They make you visible to leaders within the company and to top people outside as well. They connect you to career opportunities and provide air cover when you encounter trouble. When it comes to opening doors, they don't stop with one promotion: They'll see you to the threshold of power.'*

You'll remember sponsors from the Networking Dream Team in Chapter 4. By leveraging their own career capital and political influence, sponsors can take you to the top. ~~They put their reputation up instead of yours, so you can borrow their credibility and trust.~~ Of course, you've got to deliver stellar performance to honour their patronage. But the upsides are huge.

The involvement of a sponsor on your behalf means almost guaranteed promotions, high-profile projects, pay increases and huge career capital.[7]

20. Avoid the 'one mentor' approach

Any advantage you seize that helps you excel in your work will (a) build your reputation and (b) give you major career capital. This is where your network is vital. Yet the traditional advice to get a mentor is not the answer.

As you move up the ladder, the stuff you need to know and do increases massively. And the expectations, the complexity, the pressure and the responsibilities multiply. In an increasingly complex and demanding world, you need multiple inputs to cope. Like a unicorn, the legendary 'perfect' mentor or coach does not exist.

Realistically, what one person could cover all the online and 'in person' reputational facets you have to master? Who could know all the people you need to know? Who could be everything you need to create a career of fulfilment, significance and influence? Nobody.

---

[7]You'll find a Sponsor Manifesto in the Reputation Vault. Take a look. Have a read. Go bag a sponsor.

One mentor is great but not enough. It used to be, but no longer. You need a holistic approach featuring a range of advocates and supporters. As you're beginning to appreciate, you need a PBA or Personal Board of Advisors.

21. Create your own personal board of advisors (PBA)

Look at the top tennis players and athletes. They talk about entourage. They talk about team. They know it takes an army of coaches and experts to make a champion. As the African proverb says, '*it takes a village to raise a child*'.

That's why the accepted wisdom for modern leaders and top talent is to have a Personal Board of Advisors (PBA). Or often called your Personal Board of Directors. Your board's role is to give you feedback, insight, support and advocacy in your career quest.

As you transition into leadership and more responsibility, you need an inner circle of advisors that are fit for purpose. To avoid being out of the loop, your only option is to gain access through the minds of others. A team approach will also amplify your contribution and your reputation.

Such an approach has many benefits, including access to valuable resources, brains, creativity, support, feedback, prestige and opportunities. All massive upsides for you. Remember: it takes a village.

12 Great benefits of your PBA

A PBA has so many upsides, it's a no-brainer to assemble yours. Its benefits should outweigh any discomfort you have in (a) networking and (b) asking for help. Your benefits include:

1. **Resources**. They'll signpost you to good books, useful sites and other prized assets.

2. **Brains**. You're going to get killer advice, perspective and insight.
3. **Creativity**. You can't get enough fresh ideas and new/better ways of thinking.
4. **Support**. Life can be tough. Shit happens. Encouragement will help you get through.
5. **Feedback**. You need people to tell it to you straight and hold you accountable.
6. **Fast-track**. PBAs make things happen quicker so you get accelerated career progression.
7. **Inside-track**. Who wouldn't want introductions to interesting people and projects?
8. **Answers**. You get a sounding board to make big decisions or navigate big transitions.
9. **No FOMO**. Because you've covered bases, there is less likelihood of career regrets and FOMO (fear of missing out).
10. **Prestige**. You dine at higher tables thanks to more elevated and influential networking.
11. **Profile**. Welcome to an enhanced profile and a better reputation by association.
12. **Opportunities**. Your PBA will open doors to prime jobs and interesting opportunities, and can endorse your candidacy for otherwise impossible roles.

Where else could you get this kind of help and intel? Of course, you've got to earn it and work for it (which I'll show you later). For now, let's get building it.

• *Step one: Choosing your PBA*

In picking your board, you've got to exercise care. This is not a place for you and your mates to hang out. That's somewhere else. This is a career strategy. It's a networking thing to leverage the power of people to grow your reputation and your career capital.

You've probably got a network of 800–1,000 people if you're an average executive or professional. Out of those, at least 50 could fulfil a role on your board. How do you choose? Here are 12 valuable rules or guidelines for choosing the right people to help you:

1. **Go for diversity**. Consider different levels – your boss is not always the best person to have on the board. Include people from different industries, backgrounds, experiences and personalities. You don't just want people like you. I promise you!
2. **Go for values over roles**. Roles can sound grand and important. But you often get a better fit by choosing people who share your values. You're also looking for people who can offer the right kind of support, perspective, insight, skills and connections. It's not just about job titles. Think about the person.
3. **Keep it fresh**. People and circumstances need change. Always be looking for new members. It shakes up existing ones and mitigates any resignations or blow ups that leave you short.
4. **Offer value in exchange**. Later you'll learn some great ways to give back, but for now think of doing your board favours, giving them your time or doing research for them. Think how you can offer exposure, intro them to good people and endorse their brilliance publicly.
5. **Think back**. Reflect on who has a track record of helping you in the past. If they've done it before, they'll probably do it again.
6. **Think forward**. Look at your network and ask yourself who you would like to play a greater role in your life.
7. **Be realistic**. There is no perfect person who has it all. The gravitas. The influence. The craving to help a rising star like you. Home in on the desired qualities of each candidate and focus on why you want them on your board. Remember this is a team, not an individual, so any shortfall in their credentials can be made up by others.

8. **Separate business and personal**. If you want tips on parenting, handling bereavement, health stuff or more personal issues, consider assembling a PBA for precisely that stuff. But best not to mix it with your career and work stuff.

9. **Have an odd number of people**. Five or seven is ideal. Not only do things get a little unwieldy after that, but when you want a vote on any particular issue, there's little chance of a stalemate.

10. **Know before you ask**. Ideally you won't be asking people you don't know to come onto your board. #awkward. What's the incentive for them? So build the relationship first. Get to know them and ensure they know you.

11. **Choose people you trust**. Since you're going to be open and vulnerable with your PBA, you need to trust them. Despite their brilliance or influence, they are a bad fit if they don't share your values. When you know they have your interests at heart, they become a prime candidate.

12. **Fit your board to your needs**. The best PBA for you will match your PDP (personal development plan). What do you need to take your career to the next level? Fit the personnel to the gaps. The board make up may change, but who do you need for this season in your life? Some celebrity guru may be a coup to land but you're probably not ready for them just yet.

- *Step two: Recruiting your PBA*

You kinda know who you're after and why. Each one brings something to the party. You trust them, rate them and like them.

How do you make the ask? In a nutshell, you're going to say how you admire them and value their opinion. You're going to ask if they'd be open to connecting once in a while to give you feedback and share ideas. And you're going to thank them when they say yes.

You'll probably only get one shot at this. It's a delicate ask. An unusual request that they won't face every day. Even if they're currently mentoring people, they likely won't have been asked to be on somebody's PBA before. To elicit a 'yes', considered wisdom favours a three-step approach:

1. **Compliment**. Open with a tribute, an offering of praise. When used properly, flattery is a useful tool to court demi-gods. Say why you like them or admire them. Mention what's caught your notice. You might open with *'Do you mind if I ask you something? I've always liked the way you X ... .'* Or *'I've got a question to ask you. See, I've always admired how you've been really good at X ...'*

2. **Explain**. Tell them what you're doing and why. Explain how you're looking to kick on with your career and have some ambitious plans. And you recognize the importance of connecting with high level influential people. Say how you're putting together a Personal Board of Advisors (or Directors, whichever sounds best to them) to help you.

3. **Invite**. Ask them if they would consider taking one of the seats on your board. Say how honoured you would be if they would consider helping you on an informal basis. They may be flattered and even curious. They will naturally wonder what this entails. So outline what their commitment might be. Add that it would just mean being able to pick up the phone to them every now and again. Or take them to coffee or lunch once a quarter. Then wait for their hopefully positive response.

- *Step three: Making the PBA 'ask'*

You've got to make your invitation warm, welcoming and enticing. These people have egos and they usually want to help if they can. You've just got to make it easy for them. Using the rules in Step Two, here are three sample power scripts you can use to make the ask:

'Jim, I'd like to put a proposition to you. I'd really like you to be my mentor, which basically means we meet every three months wherever you like for as long as you

can spare and I pick up the food and drink tab. All you then do is let me ask you questions and give me advice. What do you think?'

'Julie, can I ask you a question? I'd love you to be on my personal board of advisors, and what that means is we meet a couple of times a year, I take you out for a meal of your choice and you let me pick your brains. Would you be open to that?'

'Kris, I've got something cheeky to ask you. We've known each other a while and I've always loved the way you've _____. I'm putting together my personal board of advisors and I'd love you to be on it. All that means is I can pick up the phone to you every couple of months for 20 minutes and get your best thinking on any career issues I might be going through. I've even come up with a few ways I can help you in return. How does that sound?'

If you've chosen the right person and asked in the right way, you've probably just recruited your first board member. Some may say no. You may have a hit-list of 20 to ask, so you can afford some 'turn-downs'. If you get a 'yes', fix up a first meet or call. If it's a 'no', then chalk it up to 'right idea, wrong time' and with a thank you for them even considering it, move on.

- *Step four: Running your PBA*

It's natural that you would think a Personal Board of Advisors meets frequently in person as a group like a regular board. That might happen, but that's not what this is. Your advisors probably don't know each other and might never even meet. That's natural. After all, they come from diverse backgrounds and it's unlikely their paths will cross.

1. **Meet in person or remotely**. You can do a Skype video chat, a phone call or similar. You can even record such calls (ask for their permission) for a personal record and to save you writing lots of notes. Alternatively, a face-to-face meeting over coffee or lunch (you pay) works well.

2. **Convene full meetings or do one-to-ones**. You could get your whole PBA or parts of it together. More likely, and certainly more convenient, is to pick them off one by one as and when needed.

3. **Check in regularly**. You could agree on a monthly, quarterly or annual chat or meet. Whatever is practical for them. You should also get permission to contact 'on the fly'. Something might just come up that they can speak on with authority and clarity.

4. **Issue agendas**. Consider what you want to learn from them. They might drop pearls of wisdom into your lap. But the best mentors work to a curriculum. Your curriculum. Don't waste their time. What would you like their feedback on? Let them know what they're walking into. Share in advance any questions, challenges or discussion points you'd like to cover. This respects their valuable time and gives them time to prepare.

5. **Report back**. Update them on your progress after meetings. Tell them about your wins and outcomes. Inform them of any decisions and action you've taken as a result of (or despite) their input.

6. **Give back**. Keep asking how you can help them. See later for tons of ways to even up the score. There are lots of clever ways to incentivize demi-gods to want to help you. You've just got to be creative and intentional.

7. **Reward spontaneously**. These people are devoting a part of their busy life and considerable expertise for your benefit. So well-chosen gifts, hand-written thank you cards and mentions of how great they are to others are usually very well received.

8. **Pick up the tab**. Make sure you always pay for the beer, coffee and food wherever it features. If it's at their office, bring food and drink into meetings if appropriate.

9. **Respect their time**. Be courteous with their schedule and pressures. Meet them where it's good for them. It might be at a conference you both attend. It's expected that they 'play at home' so be prepared to travel.

10. **Keep it meaty**. Focus your meetings on the big things, not small trivialities. You're not there to shoot the breeze. They're probably not

interested in that office quibble. They couldn't care less about the minor fall-out with you and your partner. Stay on the meaty topics for best results.

There's an epic PBA Manifesto in the Reputation Vault with your name on it. It gives you more on these benefits. You get tips on choosing, recruiting and running your PBA. Go get it.

Summary: Personal board toolbox

This is your Personal Board Toolbox. You know that who you associate with will have a huge impact on your life, your opportunities, your bank account and your choices.

For that reason, you've developed some potentially useful relationships. You've even begun sorting and classifying. But hold on. It's not a numbers game. You can't just count your conversations. You've got to make your conversations count.

Back in the day, when I was selling private medical insurance for a global healthcare company, I did a lot of networking. And I wasn't very good at it. In a two-year period I attended 126 business events. Think about how many that is a week. I also spent thousands of dollars on breakfast meetings, business lunches, and all kinds of memberships and conferences. I won NO business. Sure, it felt like I was busy, but I was making every networking mistake imaginable.

In the end I raised my game and became world class. Just by learning stuff, watching people do it well and learning my craft. You don't need to waste that time and go through that pain. You know how your network feeds your reputation. The more people you know, the more will know you.

You're in a much better position to articulate the kind of help you want from your network. And you appreciate how to leverage it for career capital through your PBA – Personal Board of Advisors. You recognize that one mentor or coach is okay but not enough. Tough times require team approaches.

Only a sponsor can wield enough power to act alone for you. Even then, you'll accelerate their efforts with a dream team of trusted people. And trust is important. Asking for help (which you have to do) can be seen as a sign of weakness. So your vulnerability and openness needs protecting in high-trust relationships.

To leverage the help of demi-gods and VIPs, you need some kind of give-back. A 'value for value' exchange. To leverage the help of your peers, you might just need an informal contra deal.

It is possible to manage bigger and bigger networks. Technology and online platforms help you massively with that. But a focus on quality vs quantity will allow you to make meaningful touch points with the people that count. Through it all, keep your network fresh and primed. Lose the deadwood. *The juice is not worth the squeeze.*

Chapter 9

Your Professional Toolbox: Performance

'Being highly skilled used to set you apart. Now it just qualifies you to play. GOOD gets you in the game. GREAT gets you on the podium.'

– Rob Brown

Performance – delivery – credibility

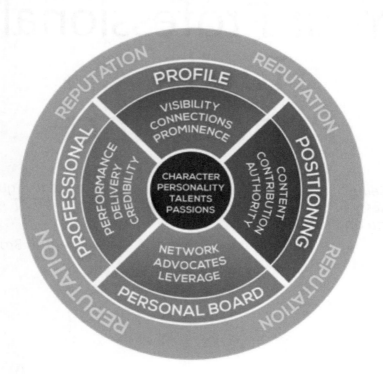

This Reputation Toolbox features strategies to enhance your credibility in the working environment. They communicate to the people that matter just how good you are in role and how much you have to offer the company that few others can. People have forced their way to the top by showing phenomenal progress in just one or two of these.

You'll see a ton of professional and personal development initiatives to grow and upskill you. They'll help you hone your craft and turbo-boost your skills. They give you hints, tips and ideas to make you slicker, better and more respected in your field.

Some strategies are business based and professional in nature. They encourage you to **do a great job**. Before you can think about being a celebrity, an authority or a strong personal brand, you've got to get the basics right. One of the best ways to get on in a company is to keep hitting your targets. Keep delivering on your plan.

You might be all over the internet and have a following of millions, but if you're just mediocre in your role, the fame doesn't count for a whole lot. In short, hit targets and 'make plan'. Deliver with excellence and attitude.

Other strategies may seem more personal. They suggest ideals to live up to. Wise words for character building or commands to enhance your personality traits. You exploit them by thinking, seeing, feeling and being certain things. These are attributes you need to BE and HAVE in order to get people talking about you in the right way.

There are plenty of character and personality based attributes that will attract others to you and get you noticed. You don't need them all. In fact, you never could have them all. But pick a few that you can relate to and resonate with you. In short, keep it real and be you.

1. Be values driven

Stick to your principles. Short cuts and hacks can be legitimate and worthy. But you'll regret sacrificing your principles for short-term and even ill-gotten gain. Look back at the Core Values Exercise in Chapter 3 and your Reputation Game Plan.

Maintain your integrity and your character. This is the sturdy foundation your reputation is built on. Know what you stand for and stick to it. This is your moral compass.

With all progress comes compromise. At times you'll be asked to lay down your personal values to reach your professional goals. It's one thing being a winner and a leader. It's another being a winner and a leader that others will follow and respect. Do the right thing, even if it means you get there a little slower. You'll sleep better at night and your reputation will be preserved.

To build the right reputation, you need to make the right decisions. To make the right decisions, you need the right moral compass and the right grounding. You do this through your values, which come from your character. Take some time to think about what you stand for and what your guiding principles will be. These will be the rock around which your mad, swirling world of business will revolve. Values and principles help you to stand firm in tough times. This virtually assures a solid reputation.

2. Be action oriented

Talk is cheap. Too many people talk about it but few take action. Reflection and discussion are all good, but it's your actions that you'll be measured by. Could this be a reputational thrust for you? If you become known for making things happen and turning plans into reality, then you'll develop some serious career capital.

As Henry Ford said: 'You can't build a reputation on what you are going to do.' It's not enough to be nice or friendly. Get things started. Build some momentum. Don't be seen as just a planner or a ditherer.

3. Be prolific

This describes someone who is fruitful and highly productive. People who do a lot of things generally build a good reputation. Get things done, make things happen and be productive if you want to develop a strong reputation. Picasso produced incredible quantities of art, including drawings, paintings and sculpture. *The Guinness Book of World Records* declares Picasso to be the most prolific painter who ever lived.

To be prolific, you need to be productive. To be productive, you need to be disciplined. To be disciplined you need to be focused. What are you focusing on to be prolific? Prolific people are producers. They create things. They have an exhaustive output. If you are dynamic with your thoughts and ideas, and have channels to put them out there, you can build a formidable reputation.

4. Be passionate

Passion is contagious. When you love what you do, people want to know you and be around you. Passion is infectious! Passion is a differentiator. Passion is purpose! When you say you love your work, people take notice. It makes you stand out. It gets you chosen, hired or promoted.

If you love what you do, make sure people know about it. There are so many ways you can show people you are passionate about your job, your calling, your position, your company. Think about how you pick up the phone to people. Those everyday touch-points are opportunities for you to show people how passionate you are about your job, your business or your calling.

5. Be persistent

Persistence is bouncing back from adversity. Picking yourself up, dusting yourself down and starting again. Simply keeping going. Steve Jobs was always convinced that about half of what separates the successful from the non-successful is pure perseverance.

When you stick it out, hang around, keep on going, overcome adversity and stay in the game, it makes you better as a person. Perseverance and persistence gives you enough time to make a name for yourself that people will take notice of. It takes a few years but eventually you'll be famous.

Many a promising reputation has faltered under duress and because of obstacles. As the old proverb says, *smooth seas do not make skilful sailors.* Some people just develop a world-class reputation by sticking around. It's not easy to become an overnight sensation. The highest reputed people are often the ones who have longevity.

You endure, you last, you stay. You overcome, you persist. When your competition falls by the wayside, you remain. People buy certainty. Knowing you've 'been around' and will continue to be around gives people that certainty.

6. Be resilient

Mental toughness is a component of executive presence. Mentally strong people are given positions of influence because they can cope. You fall down, you get back up. You fail, you learn, you succeed. Decide today to be tenacious, resilient and mentally strong.

The ability to bounce back after a setback is something very few have. You're realistic. You know there'll be trials and temptations, adversity and challenges. They say tough times come and go, but tough people stay. Be strong, dust yourself down and regroup as quickly as you can. You can bitch, moan, whine and wallow, but what good does that really do?

When you build a good reputation by bouncing back, people will stop attacking you. Decide where and how you fell short and learn the lessons. Skill up, 'man up' and go again. Make sure it doesn't happen again by being stronger and more prepared.

7. Be quick

Speed stuns. If you're highly productive, ruthlessly efficient and very action oriented, then you'll get stuff done faster than most. To be quick, you have to be organized, disciplined and systemized. You need a laser-like focus to stay on task and get things done.

You'll hit deadlines, often early. You'll under-promise and over-deliver. You'll soon make a name for yourself as the number-one obvious choice for that which you do. Distractions will come thick and fast, but if you can get more done in two hours than most people do in a day, you'll attract a lot of positive attention and interesting opportunities. This 'greed for speed' will carve out a phenomenal reputation for you as someone that gets stuff done, and gets it done quickly. People will come to you because you take action and you deliver results. You'll seize the moment. You'll act quickly.

> *'It is impossible to travel faster than the speed of light, and certainly not desirable, as one's hat keeps blowing off.'*
> *Woody Allen*

8. Be generous

When you offer your expertise, time and knowledge, people think well of you. When you bring in an extra coffee, doughnut or soda for someone, you create allies all over the place. It creates huge goodwill. It fills up the emotional bank account. You can draw on this later if you screw up and need forgiveness. Or if you've got a problem and need a favour.

9. Ask great questions

Be curious. It's the inquisitive people that solve the most problems. And the bigger the problems you solve, the more you get paid. Inventors and innovators are curious. Entrepreneurs and leaders are curious. They constantly ask questions of themselves and those around them. Curious people strive to make things better. They aim to live a life of significance that often comes from serving others and solving problems. Do all you can to elicit The Four P's of People:

1. **Pain** – where are they hurting?
2. **Problems** – what challenges and obstacles are in their way?
3. **Projects** – what are they working on right now?
4. **Plans** – what are their goals and dreams?

The answers to all of these vital questions will uncover huge opportunities for you. When you can offer help and advice to people, you'll develop a great reputation. So ask questions. Good questions. Better questions.

Get curious and find out what people really want. Then give it to them and they'll love you for it.[1]

10. Be visionary

Set lofty goals. Think big. You may never be world famous. But the higher you reach, the higher you will go. Your goals and your potential will not be served by you thinking small. The difference you want to make lies on the other side of some big dreams. So stretch yourself with something big that will make your good name great.

11. Be confident

Develop self-belief. Other people won't believe in you unless you believe in yourself. Make sure you know what you are talking about. Then sound as if you know what you are talking about. Be assertive. When you're confident in yourself, you'll win the confidence of others.

Confident people back themselves. They have developed a strong mental toughness and work well under pressure. They handle stress well and can be counted on in tight situations. Much of this comes from powerful self-belief and inner confidence. And it's very attractive and magnetic to have!

Confidence in your own abilities is a very compelling trait. You'll draw people to you when you demonstrate a positive outlook and show an 'appetite for the fight'. Of course, you will mess up and you will get things wrong. Many times you will fail. The important thing is not failure, but

---

[1]You'll find a Questions Manifesto waiting in the Reputation Vault for you. It's about the power of great questions and contains a ton of really powerful ones to set you apart when you're around leaders and demi-gods.

your attitude to it and how soon you get over it. Don't allow failure to keep you down. You must get up fast.

12. Develop empathy

Do you really care? If you strive to cultivate a caring personality, you will generate a caring business. More than that, you will have an outstanding 'go-to' reputation as somebody who holds the best interest of others rather than working for purely self-serving reasons.

Properly serving and looking after your employees, customers, clients, stakeholders is basic. Caring about people is often about the intangibles. The stuff you can't put a finger on. The stuff you do above and beyond your core level of service or job description.

It's a given that your product, service or performance will be good. That's the benchmark. What you do beyond that to provide an experience that delights is what shows you really care. Going 'above and beyond' is what makes a good name great! There's very little traffic on the 'extra mile' because very few people go there.

13. Aspire to high standards

When your expectations are high, the quality of your work and your inter-actions will be equally high. As a result, your reputation will soon be exceptional. Striving for excellence is something that most people strug-gle with. It takes effort and exertion. Such people want to do just enough to get by. They ask: 'How can I get this done with the minimum of effort?' If that's you, you'll have to work hard for your reputation.

There's nothing wrong with wanting to work smarter and minimize your effort. But at the expense of quality, excellence or high standards? Decide today to make the effort to go just a little further than your colleagues or your competition. You don't have to be much better than them. Just a little. It's the equivalent of a horse winning a race by just a nose but claiming ten times the prize money of the horse that comes second. You gain a good name and a powerful reputation by doing a great job – something more than ordinary or average.

14. Be reliable

This is simply doing what you say you're going to do. Keeping commitments creates huge relationship capital. Be congruent. Align your promises with your actions. When you keep coming through, people are drawn to you. It builds massive trust. Nobody leans on the flakey person who bails at late notice, makes excuses and misses deadlines. Unreliability is the number one career-limiting habit.[2]

Be true to your word. Go to invitations you accept. Show up when you promise to. The most reliable people manage themselves and their time very well. Know when to say no so you don't get overloaded. If you want to improve your reliability, start making small commitments to people. 'I'll have that with you by close of business Tuesday.' Follow through on them and you'll get better with the bigger things.

15. Listen well

When you hear people out, they feel included and worthy. This creates significant reputational stock. When you ask them how they're doing and really mean it, people know. When you enquire about their weekend because you really want to know, people can tell. By developing your listening skills, you'll also open yourself up to lots of new ideas and opportunities. You can never really listen too much. It's a skill worth honing.

16. Work your business card

It's all about how and when to use them, and what the best business cards have that the others don't. Remember: your business card is your calling card. It's an extension of your personal brand. It's very often all that's left

---

[2]http://www.eatyourcareer.com/2011/06/careerlimiting-habits-guilty/

of you when you leave the room. So it's vital you work it and use it to stay memorable and keep in touch. So here are three simple tips to get you started with using your business card more effectively:

1. **Be proactive and ask for people's cards**. Don't wait for people to offer their card.
2. **Write relevant information on the card, such as the main point you discussed**. These notes will make a big difference when following up with that person.
3. **Use your card to get a card**. The card you receive is more important than the one you give, because it gives you their contact details and 'permission to contact'. Offering your card to them first is a useful way of having them reciprocate. *The card you get beats the card you give in any card game.*

When you become more adept with business cards, you'll begin building the contacts and the network that will define your reputation.

17. Be different with your voicemail

If someone has taken the trouble to call, don't just tell them you're out or away. At least consider having a professional message, dated and recorded daily. It takes a few seconds and a little discipline, and creates a strong impression. You need to be prepared for these situations.

Could you mention where you are, or a project you're working on? Could you say when you'll be back and available? Could you put some passion in your voice? Could you make it funny or memorable? The answer to all of these is yes. So use this moment to make a positive impression and add some reputation points.

18. Ask for help and advice

Nobody builds a reputation for anything significant on their own. You cannot afford to wait until people volunteer for your cause. You have to ask.

You may have heard it said that the answer to every question you don't ask is 'no'. So what have you got to lose?

Just because someone is famous, superior or some kind of guru, doesn't mean they won't help you. Who knows what might lie on the other side of a courageous request for help? The help and advice of the world's most incredible people is available if you can find a way to ask.

Become known for asking for help. Not in a needy way, but in a way that says you're not too big or arrogant to reach out. When you word your request in a deferential way, you'll get a better response AND build your reputation simultaneously. A useful tip is to compliment someone before you ask for their advice. It's so hard to say 'no' to and they think more of you for asking.

19. Do written goals

This is a great habit to get into. We've done you a Goals Manifesto to go deeper into this topic. Writing down your goals and reviewing them often keeps you on task and maintains momentum. Goals are very misunderstood yet very powerful.

The top performers set and achieve a range of goals. It's a good thing for you to know exactly how goals work. The psychology, the theories and the right ways to use them.

It's a fact that people who achieve more, set goals. If you want to develop a track record for getting things done, tackling big projects and achieving incredible things, get writing your goals down.

20. Set minor achievable goals

Nothing boosts your confidence like a good outcome or an achieved goal. Positive results make you feel good and exhort you to greater things. Here are 10 small work goals you could set and achieve without too much stretch:

1. Volunteer for a project or committee.
2. Attend a conference or networking event.
3. Buy three people a coffee or soda this week.
4. Invite somebody to an event.
5. Organize a social event for colleagues.
6. Clear your inbox.
7. Learn a new computer skill or program.
8. Teach yourself to type.
9. Say hello and smile to 10 people before breakfast.
10. Make 10 phone calls before 10 am.

You get the idea. The list is endless. None of these is major. But all give you confidence to do again, do bigger and do better.

21. Become great with your time

William Penn said: 'Time is what we want most, but what we use worst.' Time poverty is the biggest single problem facing most professionals today. There is probably no other skill that you can learn that will give you a 'bigger bang for your buck' than to become great at managing your time. When you become disciplined and focused with your tasks, you become ruthlessly efficient and powerfully effective.

You create the time and space to be creative and to work on the 'important but not urgent' stuff like reputation building. There are loads of books on time management. Invest in some and begin adopting some great skills and habits to boss your time more effectively. Then you can get more done, wow more people and create more career capital.

22. Finish things

Get stuff done and over the line. People like people who get things done. Become known as a completer and finisher. Hit deadlines early. Don't wait for people to chase you up for things.

23. Avoid comparisons

There's always going to be somebody better than you at something and somebody worse. Comparisons rarely help. When you compare yourself to people better than you, you might start feeling down or inferior. If worse than you, you might feel smug, complacent or even arrogant. If equal, you might get competitive or adversarial.

None of these emotions really help you. IF you're going to compare yourself to someone, compare all of your life, ups, downs, failings, strengths and circumstances with all of theirs. Then ask if you'd rather be them or you. When you look into the whole of people's lives enviously, you find there are plenty of things going on there that you'd rather not swap for your life. Back yourself. Be happy being you. Avoid comparisons.

24. Think in increments

You don't have to be brilliant today. Just a bit closer to it than yesterday. You don't have to master something in a week. You just need to nudge it along and keep going step by step. This is called thinking in increments.

Darren Hardy's brilliant book *The Compound Effect* talks up this concept. Small, smart choices add up to big differences over time. Don't be too downhearted if you don't see huge progress over short time scales. A little bit each day will make it happen eventually. It's the only way to take on big projects and huge audacious goals without giving up after slow progress.

25. Practise, practise, practise

All good art, skills, ideas and performances need crafting. View your contribution as the tip of an arrow. It's where you will pierce the busy thick skin of corporate life to make your mark. It's where you will gain entry into the noisy worlds and busy schedules of the senior decision makers in your organization.

You've still got to follow up and follow through though. You've got to get their attention, and then wow them. You've got to sell your wares and promote your message. That takes skill, practice and drive.

You gotta get good! If you've got some kind of calling in your life, or a passionate pursuit that excites and absorbs you, then you're blessed. If you've got an abundance of talent and you're oozing natural ability where you don't really have to try to be brilliant, you're a fabulous and enviable freak.

For the rest of us, we're going to have to work at it. You must deepen your knowledge and invest in your skills. You must practise your art, think deeply about your area of speciality and work hard to produce good stuff. It was T. Harv Eker that said 'every master was once a disaster', so keep working on yourself.

With a strong self-development ethic, you're going to improve in whatever you set your mind to. This builds skill and expertise that helps you stand out. It's precious career capital that you can trade for influence, career choice and authority marketing.

Cal Newport says people fare better in their careers if they adopt a mindset of 'What can I offer the world vs what can the world offer me?' Strive to constantly get better. Your ideas will be better (slicker and clearer), your skills will be better (honed and battle ready) and your contribution will be better.

26. Take seminars, courses and classes

Your continuing education should be life-long to keep you ahead of the chasing pack. Many top professionals invest around 10% of their annual income back into professional development. You can get stuff in a one-hour seminar with an expert that's taken them a lifetime to learn. That's got to be a great use of your time.

Knowledge is power, particularly when it's applied to helping people and solving problems. Get armed and dangerous by taking in the very best learning you can to raise your game and set yourself apart. Otherwise you'll just be and look like everyone else. And that's not good for a stand-out reputation.

27. Read more

Most people don't read. Crazy, eh? Not you, obviously, because you're reading this. Look for books, magazines and articles that address your industry, niche and type of work. You won't read them all. But even skimming through them and noting the key points will get you ahead of the game.

Read extensively if you really want to become an authority and stand-out thought leader. It's been said that where you end up five years from now will depend on the people you've got around you and the books you've read. If you're not reading and learning, you're going backwards in today's fast-paced world. Today's readers are tomorrow's leaders.

Put another way, learners are earners. Investing in yourself will increase your knowledge, your expertise and your skills. People will seek you out because you know stuff and because you'll know where to find stuff.

28. Share your personal development library

When people see the kind of things you read (even if you have not read every single page of every single book) they will respect you for your knowledge and commitment to learning. There's nothing wrong with making your library public. Share great books in person, at meetings, on LinkedIn and through social media channels.

Lend books to others. Show them your library and invite them to choose a couple they'd like to borrow. Get your phone out and take a photo of them with the book. That way you remember who borrowed it. It's also a great reason to re-connect by sending them the image and asking 'how's the book going?'

Books are not meant to just sit on a shelf. Share the knowledge, share the love and share the learning. It makes you interesting. It makes you engaging. And it makes you better. It's funny how the poorest people often have the biggest TV screens and the smallest libraries. Go and figure that one out!

29. Learn new skills

In this fast-moving world, your skills can become obsolete quite quickly. Skill is the ability to do something well. It's expertise and applied ability. Other words are knack, craft, proficiency, dexterity. Skill is not talent. You're born with that. It's what God gives you.

Skill is what you give yourself. The things you become good at. Trouble is, the stuff you were doing a few years ago might be irrelevant today. The things you knew five years ago might be holding you back right now. The need to stay fresh and right up to date with your skill is vital for success in business today.

You need to upskill and stay ahead of the game. Without the right skills, your ability to develop the reputation you want may be severely hindered. Even simple things, like teaching yourself to touch type or mastering some new technology, might mean you don't get left behind.

To master the basics of a new language, you need to learn a vocabulary of around 2,500 of the most frequently used words. If you break that down to three new words a day for a couple of years, it's doable, right? Whether it's understanding Twitter and Facebook, mastering your mobile phone, building your networking skills or memorizing some great questions to ask influential people, upskill now. Your reputation will be so enhanced!

'I am always doing that which I cannot do, in order that I may learn how to do it.'

Pablo Picasso

30. Learn smarter

What are you doing to learn better ways to learn? Reading is great, but how is your speed reading? Listening to audio books and programmes is brilliant, but can you go through them on double speed? Most of the podcast apps now allow you to vary the listening speed AND cut out silences.

You can watch YouTube videos at enhanced speeds and get through more, faster. You can get executive book summaries to save you hours and get the key points without having to read the whole thing. The more you can learn, the more you can earn, as the saying goes. So learn smart and get more professional development done.

31. Coach and mentor others

When you teach others, it makes you better. It drives your skills and knowledge deeper into yourself. It keeps you sharp and current. You have to stay ahead of those whose lives you are speaking to.

Mentoring or helping others also gives you your biggest chance to be persuasive and influential, and that makes for a great reputation. Mentoring others is the kind of thing that gets you talked about and mentioned when people win awards. They credit you with their success. They rave about you to their network. That makes for a great reputation and strong career capital.

'The greatest good you can do for another is not just to share your riches but to reveal to him his own.'

Benjamin Disraeli

32. Deliver great service

Customer or client service is a rather neglected area of business life. The companies and people that get it right can make a huge difference to their repeat and referral business and to the loyalty of their patrons.

Your customer is also your boss, your team and your stakeholder. Treating people right makes a big impression and creates the stories that build a world-class reputation. Whatever good service looks like, make sure you're on it.

Check out the concept of Critical Non-Essentials (CNEs) by an Australian dentist called Paddi Lund. CNEs are things that are critical to providing a good experience but not essential to the basic product or service. CNEs are not strictly necessary to deliver, but provide delight and differentiation in what you offer.

For instance, Paddi Lund addresses his patients by name when they arrive for treatment. They get their own waiting room with fresh flowers, sugar-free dental buns and fresh coffee. None of this has anything to do with filling your teeth, but it gets people talking. It makes you 1% different, and that's enough to make your good service great.

33. Keep current

Staying on top of what's important is a good thing. It means you know what's going on and you don't get left behind. Subscribe to email newsletters, blogs, news feeds and specialized publications. This keeps you ahead of the game and starts to mark you as an expert. They say an expert is someone who knows just 10% more than their audience!

When you start thinking about what you're keeping current with, you become a thought leader. So listen to podcasts and tune into webinars and teleseminars. Use mobile apps and gadgets. These kinds of mediums deliver very up-to-date information. Double speed. You must develop personally and professionally to cultivate and maintain your reputation.

34. Be externally aware

It's so easy to get absorbed in your daily to do list. It's like the external world doesn't exist. Yet there are new, interesting, disruptive and engaging ideas out there that you need to know about. More than that, your company needs to know about them.

Every time you bring fresh ideas and perspective to your company, you add value. You create career capital. You provide valuable 'bring-back' for your network. It might be as simple as following seven external thought leaders, business figures or companies on Twitter or LinkedIn. It could be meeting up with a few people in different industries and asking 'what's new?'

> 'Unless leaders are connecting inside and outside, and inhaling different conversations, they cannot breathe ideas back into the business.'
>
> Phil Jones, MD of Brother UK

35. Keep your sales skills sharp

Your reputation will bring people to you, but you will still have to clinch the deal and close the sale. You might be a reluctant salesman/saleswoman, but the highest-paid people in professional life tend to be those who sell well. Everyone in life is selling something. It could be your arguments, your excuses, your vision, your dream, your strategy, your opinion, your goal or even yourself.

Honing your sales skills is vital in persuading and influencing others to do what you want them to do. It's crucial in driving change and changing behaviours. If you can improve your sales skills by just 10%, you'll make a massive impact not only on your good name, but on your ability to leverage that good name for fame and fortune.

36. Get good in meetings

Office meetings are great opportunities for you to build your reputation and let people know you're an asset. Here are a few quick tips to get good in meetings.

- **Come prepared**. Get the agenda, do some prep and be ready for everything. Just being organized shows diligence and professionalism.
- **Ask an early question**. Even something vague like *'will this scale?'* or *'So, where are we at this?'* will get people thinking.
- **Quiz the intellectuals**. Some people like to show off in meetings. Everyone knows it. You can gain huge kudos by keeping the show-offs humble. Hit them with something that's hard to answer, like *'yes, I hear what you're saying but what's the real problem we're trying to solve here?'* or *'so where are you up to with that project?'*
- **Make notes**. It makes you look smart even if it's a shopping list. But seriously, if you can make good notes on what's happening, you can share with people who missed the meeting and play back key points if things get confusing. Makes you look good.

We can't avoid meetings. But you can use them to strengthen your claim for presence and reputation.[3]

37. Improve your phone skills

The phone is a powerful weapon in modern business. Whether you're leaving messages for people on their voicemail or having live phone conversations, it pays to master the phone. Here are a few useful tips to raise your phone game:[4]

- **Use names**. Not overly so, but people always appreciate hearing their name.
- **Limit the background noise**. It sounds more professional that way.
- **Stand up when you talk**. It gives you more energy and focus.
- **Be in the moment**. Checking your emails might result in you missing something crucial.

---

[3]You can also get lots more great tips for being in and running great meetings in the special Meetings Manifesto in the Reputation Vault.
[4]You can also boost your phone skills with our Telephone Manifesto in the Reputation Vault.

- **Make important calls with good comms connections**. You may lose signal if you've got weak mobile phone coverage, or you're moving on trains, planes and cars. Not ideal.

38. Keep your energy high

Your ability to perform at a consistently high level is dependent on you having the energy to expend. Concentrating for long periods, focusing without getting distracted, cutting through problems with clarity. All this requires brain power, which requires calories.

Eat well, sleep well and stay on your game. Will power, discipline and concentration require energy and focus. Consistently high performers are well-fuelled and well-rested. So look after yourself.

39. Go first

There is power in making the first move. Can you lead by example? Be the first to try something. A new coffee place, a new software program, a new learning idea or new piece of technology. Try to be a pioneer. Suck it up and give it a go. Not only will you probably master it before others, you'll also be the person they come to for advice on making it work or feedback on how it went.

In social situations, be the first to pour the coffee in a meeting or break the ice at a social gathering. Be the first to offer your hand at a networking event or the first to reach out after a meeting. People remember the first man on the moon but not so much the second. Make an impression more often by going first.

40. Handle office politics

Playing the power game (or at least knowing who is playing it) in your work environment is vital for your reputation. Study the org chart. Discern the pecking orders and who the power players and gossipers are. Obviously try to be nice and maintain your integrity.

Follow through on your commitments and promises so nobody can accuse you of falling short. Wherever possible, mediate disagreements and build consensus. Try to be the broker. Probe personal agendas and respect territories. Don't be naive and think you can ignore the politics if you're going to be an influencer. It comes with the turf.

41. Look the part

Your appearance and physical image play a part in your reputation. If you want to be seen as promotional and leadership material, you've got to look the part. If you're unsure what to wear, check out what the leaders and people above you are wearing.

If you're going to act first class, you have to look first class. Within minutes of meeting you, a new contact will have judged your credibility on what you wear, what your hair looks like and the state of your health.

A little investment in your physical appearance (grooming and clothes) will go a long way to cementing you as professional and credible in the eyes of others. When you look right, you feel right. Being comfortable in your own skin is one of the most compelling and attractive features of another human being.

Dress codes have changed in the last 20 years. We've become less formal. Yet image is still ranked at the top in what makes somebody appear professional. Be consistent, not too flashy and don't go crazy on dress down days. Above all, remember your image is a big part of first impressions. Which set very quickly, so get it right!

42. Learn body language

Business is personal. It's all about people. Your reputation is what other people think about you. That means influencing them to do, think and say the right things.

Studying body language is a great reputation-building tactic for two reasons. First, you will become more aware of the signals you are giving out and what you are saying 'between your words'. Second, you'll be more educated about what other people are thinking through their non-verbal cues and gestures.

They say success is 'in the margins'. That means there is often very little to choose between someone who 'makes it' and someone who doesn't quite make it. The 'winners' do the things that the 'losers' don't like to do. That means getting a little education here and doing some profile raising there.

Developing an awareness of your own body language will help you do all the right things when you're out there meeting people and building relationships. It will also teach you who has presence and why. Presence enhances your reputation. What people don't say is often more important than what they do say. Wife

> *'I speak two languages – Body and English.'*
>
> Mae West

43. Be held accountable

This is especially important as you move higher up in a company. With responsibility comes power. With bigger salaries come bigger decisions. Get used to checking in with people and giving honest answers to 'how's it going?'

Appoint some mentors or peers to ask you the awkward questions like 'what's most challenging for you right now?'[5]

---

[5]We've also done a list of great accountability tips and questions in a special Accountability Manifesto in the Reputation Vault if you want to go deeper into this.

44. Be decisive

People hate ditherers, procrastinators and flakes. Become better and faster with your decision making. If you persistently hesitate on big and small calls, you'll damage your reputation. People prefer action and movement, even if it's not always the right conclusion.

Not making decisions means you'll lose out on opportunities. A fear of making the wrong choice paralyses most people. But usually the person who makes 50 quick decisions a day will outperform the one who makes 10 and delays on 40. Sometimes just making a decision brings answers that you'd never uncover if you'd delayed. Speak up and speak out. Make the call and don't dither.

45. Make sacrifices

If you want success in one area, you'll probably have to sacrifice something in another. People at the top have made huge sacrifices. You shouldn't have to sacrifice personal happiness and personal health to reach the summit. Of course you'll lose out on some opportunities because you've chosen others. Strategically chosen. But try to keep the personal stuff intact.

Winners pay a price. You may have to decide what that price is. But nobody is going to hand you your dream job on a plate. Career capital is earned, not bestowed. This is not a lottery where you get so lucky that you don't have to do any work. Luck may play a part, but it is not the whole thing. Pay the price and enjoy the success.

46. Take risks

Tom Peters famously said: 'Test fast, fail fast, adjust fast.' This is about taking risks, which also means dealing well with failures and losses. Risk-takers are innovators. They lead courageously and quickly gain a reputation for bold, brave decisions. They say if you don't risk big, then you can't win big. Play your part in developing a risk-taking culture. Just ensure that where possible your risks are strategically analysed and company aligned.

There's an old proverb that says 'nothing in life is worth having that doesn't lie on the other side of a risk'. Like the famous Dr Pepper ad, ask yourself: 'What's the worst that could happen?' Then ask: 'What's the best that could happen?' Sometimes it's a risk to play it safe, so you might as well go for it.

47. Say sorry

If you get things wrong or upset people, apologize quickly. Do it with sincerity and be ready to do it more than once. It takes a big person to humble themselves and say sorry. Yet it's one of the very best ways to rebuild a damaged reputation.

48. Manage your boss

It might sound strange to manage your boss when it's usually the other way round, but ask yourself: how easy you are to manage? Does your boss know how to motivate you? How to get the best out of you?

Like the manager of a sports team, there are different egos, personalities and talents that a boss has to elicit work product from. More than that, the best bosses know they're measured on added value. This is that discretionary effort they can elicit from you that's above and beyond your regular job description.

There are things your boss should know about you. Like when they can lean on you and what work you like doing best. It's your job to tell them. So on your next one-to-one with your line manager, ask them: *'Would it help you to know how to get the best possible out of me in my day to day role?'* Any boss worth anything would say 'sure!' If your boss says 'not really' then get a new boss or a new job.

49. Make your boss look good

This is a smart way to make yourself popular. As long as you're not so good at doing it that your boss blocks every promotion opportunity to keep you where you are. Making them shine has many benefits. It makes them think well of you, so you look good. It enhances the company, and stuff for the collective always gets back to those higher up.

It makes your boss tell others about you. It helps you stand out. It makes you more indispensable. And it makes their job easier, which again reflects well on you. Obviously it's a delicate thing. Tricky. No one likes a suck-up and if you don't watch your step, your best intentions may label you as such. Remember: the goal is not to make everyone else look bad, but to make your boss, and yourself, look good.[6]

50. Solicit feedback

Ask people how you're doing. Find out what's going on in their minds about you. It's great reputation collateral and helps you correct any unseen faults or errors in your game. They say feedback is the breakfast of champions, and it's a fact that the top performers in almost every field have coaches who are giving them feedback on all kinds of things.

Let people know that it's great to hear that you did well but you're even more keen to hear what you could improve on. Write down what they say if you can. You'll remember it better and it shows you take it seriously.

51. Respond well to criticism

You won't improve if you're not open to criticism. Become known for your willingness to accept the opinions of others on all aspects of your performance. Show people that you take ownership of mistakes and are ready to accept responsibility when you fall short. Acknowledging your errors and doing all you can to put them right are marks of a good leader.

---

[6]Don't forget there's a great Boss Manifesto waiting for you in the Reputation Vault. You'll get some really useful ways to make your boss (and thus you) look good as well as some great tips to help you manage your boss much better.

Make people feel they did the right thing in bringing it to your attention. You don't want to encourage all kind of critical chastising of your best work. But you do want to keep the lines of feedback open so you don't develop any blind spots.[7]

52. Uncover problems early

The quicker you can see what's going wrong, the quicker you can fix it. Whether it's your problem or somebody else's. Gain a reputation for diagnosing swiftly and getting to the heart of a problem. If it's going wrong, recognize the signs as early as possible.

When you spot problems early, you can save valuable time, costs and embarrassment. This is good for everyone. Checking on how things are going is a vital part of monitoring progress. Having benchmarks or milestones to know where you should be at also helps. Not everyone has a knack for project management, but certainly this aspect of clocking difficulties and hitches early is a phenomenal skill to develop.

53. Delegate well

Delegating is an art. Getting people to buy into taking on tasks and projects is something of an art. We've actually done a Delegation Manifesto. From deciding what to delegate to choosing the right people to delegate to, this leadership skill can make a huge difference to your reputation and your ability get things done.

Aside from getting more done, the upsides of delegation – like empowering others and helping them create career capital – make delegation a must for you. Sharing rewards, giving credit where due and knowing your people are all part of successful delegation. Add it to your portfolio of skills if you want to move up the career ladder.

---

[7]There's more on this in our Feedback Manifesto in the Reputation Vault, including tips on how to ask for, offer and react to feedback of all kinds.

54. Understand psychometrics

Knowing yourself and others is at the heart of leadership and reputation. The various psychometric and personality tests can be really helpful in getting a handle on people. Obviously we're all unique and all complex. But there are common traits and behaviours that make people easier to get on with and ahead of.

If the company has any involvement with testing, it's always good to get involved. See also if you can get some insight into interpreting the results. Any insight you get and develop into how to understand people better is going to make you a better leader and influencer. All great career capital and reputational collateral.

55. ~~Work hard~~

Very few people expend maximum effort. Most just do the minimum to get by. But that's not how to get maximum results. Working smart is obviously the way to go, but working hard AND smart is going to bring you the maximum return.

Of course, you're only mortal, so take care of yourself and don't overdo it. But if you're going to do something, do it right and do it well. Do the maximum and give full effort. Make your contribution count. A strong work ethic is a good thing to be known for. Plus you'll get so much more done than the average person. That's going to do your reputation the power of good.

A thought on working hard. Don't become a workaholic. That's counterproductive. There will be reasons in your job to stay late, work like a dog and get the job done. But check yourself that you're still okay 'switching off' and winding down.

'People pretend not to like grapes when the vines are too high for them to reach.'
Marguerite de Navarre

56. Work smart

Sometimes you can't work any harder. But you can work smarter. For instance, take more breaks. They say the brain focuses well for 30–90 minutes before needing a break. Trial this for yourself and see where your sweetspot is.

Work on your skills (often called sharpening the saw) so you're more efficient with tasks. Manage your time better so you get more out of every hour. Master time wasters like email and phone interruptions. Get some great systems and processes in place.[8]

57. Develop good habits

This is a fascinating area of personal development. It's said the average person develops 6–10 new habits per year. Which ones are you adopting and also dropping? A habit is something you do every day. You will be the culmination of all of your habits. Some good, some bad.

If you can get into some good routines with areas such as exercise, sleep, emails, eating, phone calls, content creating, reading and networking, you can be a world beater.[9]

Summary: Professional toolbox

You can create a reputation for any one of these. This list is not exclusive. There are thousands of personality traits, professional qualities and

---

[8] You should also check out our Work Smarter Manifesto in the Reputation Vault for more tips on working smarter.

[9] There's a special Habits Manifesto in the Reputation Vault where you'll find some great insight into exactly what habits are, how they're formed and how to use them for power and reputation.

compelling personal attributes that will make people speak favourably about you. Feel free to pick your own if your favourite is not there.

Your aim is to **become a person worth talking about**. Deliver strongly. Hit your targets. Do a great job. Be functionally strong. Keep working on yourself and your skills. All of these will help future-proof you for tomorrow's uncertain workplace. They'll also give you valuable career capital.

REFERENCES

Baber, Anne; Waymon, Lynne, *et al.* (2015) *Strategic Connections*, Amacom

Bolles, Richard Nelson (2015) *What Colour Is Your Parachute?*, Ten Speed Press

Brown, Rob (2014) 'The Personal Brand of You: What's in Your Red Box?', TEDx, https://www.youtube.com/watch?v=rGbsb6aXbzc

Cialdini, Robert (2007) *Influence: The Psychology of Persuasion*, HarperBusiness

Gladwell, Malcolm (2008) *Outliers: The Story of Success*, Penguin

Gladwell, Malcolm (2002) *The Tipping Point*, Abacus

Godin, Seth (2010) *LinchPin: Are You Indispensable?*, Piatkus

Hardy, Darren (2012) *The Compound Effect*, CDS Books

Heath, Chip and Heath, Dan (2010) *Stick – How to Change Things When Change is Hard*, Crown Business

Hewlett, Sylvia Ann (2013) *Forget a Mentor, Find a Sponsor*, Harvard Business Review Press

Hill, Linda and Lineback, Kent (2011) 'The Three Networks You Need', *Harvard Business Review*, March 2011

Ibarra, Herminia and Hunter, Mark Lee (2007) 'How Leaders Create and Use Networks', *Harvard Business Review* January 2007

McGrath, Cathleen and Zell, Deone (2002) 'Profiles of Trust: Who to Turn to and for What', *Harvard Business Review*, January 2002

McKay, Harvey (1999) *Dig Your Well before You're Thirsty*, Bantam Doubleday Dell Publishing Group

Newport, Cal (2012) *So Good They Can't Ignore – Why Skills Trump Passion in the Quest for Work You Love*, BusinessPlusUS

Prahalad, CK and Hamel, Gary (1990) 'The Core Competence of the Corporation,' *Harvard Business Review*, May–June 1990

Rath, Tom (2013) *Strengthsfinder 2.0*, Gallup Press

Rath, Tom (2016) *Vital Friends: The People You Can't Afford to Live Without*, Gallup Press

Reibstein, Professor David (2004) 'Connecting Marketing Metrics to Financial Consequences', The Wharton School

Stradtman, Lori Randall (2012) *Online Reputation Management For Dummies*, John Wiley and Sons

The Reputation Institute (2015) 'Playing to Win in the Reputation Economy'

ADDITIONAL RESOURCES

The Reputation Vault

From the desk of Rob Brown July 2016:

The Reputation Vault is an additional online resource that gives you access to all those extras that I couldn't fit into this book. It's a resource that comprises of 26 Manifestos written to compliment this book in key areas. Together, you have the perfect blueprint to help you develop your personal brand, enhance your reputation to ensure you stand out in your field, and have a successful career.

I've called them manifestos. While this is usually a word for political documents, manifestos are also seen as powerful catalysts for action. They state views, intentions, beliefs and suggestions. For the purpose of building your reputation they give you checklists, tips and strategies to flesh out many areas of the book.

They are shown here in the order that they are referenced in the book. To access *The Reputation Vault*, go to www.theRobBrown.com/Rep-Vault and enter your name and email. If prompted for a password please enter the eighth word of the third paragraph in Chapter 3, followed by the page number.

All are just a few pages long and no more than a 30-minute read. Perfect professional development for that commute, departure lounge or boring meeting!

1. The Executive Presence Manifesto

Dives into that subtle blend of gravitas, temperament, inner strength, credibility, charisma and skills that get you viewed as a player and a peer of the top people. If you want to be seen as a peer of senior influential people, you have to talk their talk and walk their walk. That needs corporate executive presence!

2. The Strengths Manifesto

Raising your reputational game by building up your weaknesses is old-world thinking. What's clear now is that the best way to clear water between you and your rivals is to focus on your strengths. This manifesto covers exactly what strengths are, how you identify them and how to exploit them for your reputational advantage!

3. The Peer Appraisal Manifesto

Finding out what people say about you can do wonders for improving yourself. Otherwise how do you know what you're good at or what to improve. Soliciting critical and honest feedback in the right way can identify your strengths and blind spots. Peer appraisal is a powerful feedback mechanism for building a world-class, stand-out reputation!

4. The Follow Up Manifesto

So you meet a 'demi-god' or VIP. Unless they're so taken with you that they hire you right there on the spot, you're probably going to need to sustain that connection. This guide will help show you ways to follow up or keep in touch after you've met some of these interesting people. When done right, they'll remember you, refer you and perhaps even recruit you!

5. The Thought Leadership Manifesto

Ever wondered what makes someone a thought leader? What do they do? What are the benefits of being a thought leader? Could you be one? Read about how to turn ideas into success and replicate what these special people do. Thought leadership creates authority status, and that's what makes you stand out!

6. The Power Script Manifesto

Trying to get what you want out of a sale, an opportunity, or a person can be difficult when you don't know exactly what to say. A power script is simply the right thing said at the right time to the right person in the right way to elicit a particular result. It's a must for critical conversations when much is at stake!

7. The Self-Promotion Manifesto

Nobody wants to sound big-headed or arrogant. Even with an army of advocates, you must learn the art of self-promotion or ethical bragging. This manifesto gives you tips and scripts for selling yourself without sounding like you're boasting. Remember some of your bestselling OF you will be done BY you. Being able to sell yourself at the right moment in time is vital if you want to be successful!

8. The Online Reputation Manifesto

How strong is your online reputation? In this online world, you can't ignore the power of the internet, social media and mobile to shape and enhance your profile – if people can't locate you online, then they may as well not be able to locate you at all. Your impact is limited if you are brilliant but anonymous. Well-kept secrets don't tend to change the world!

9. The Give-Back Manifesto

Giving back is a pathway to success in your field. People will remember you for giving back, returning favours and making contributions. It will make people want to help you and pitch you on the same level as them. This quality, when properly harnessed, allows you to engage with the demi-gods and influencers in your space!

10. The Content Creation Manifesto

Content is so important to your authority status. It's the way you disseminate your ideas, opinions and philosophies. It gives you presence and credibility. This guide helps you form a content creation strategy that gets you out there with power presence!

11. The Saying 'No' Manifesto

The ability to stay focused, do 'deep work' and stay on task is what separates the good from the great. In the midst of distractions, interruptions and impositions, you must protect your most precious of resources: time. That means saying 'no' to a range of favours and requests. This manifesto gives you a selection of strategies and scripts to do exactly that!

12. The Trust Manifesto

Like empathy, trust is a vital cornerstone of influence. When people trust you, they are more likely to refer you, endorse you and listen to you. Trust means people will buy you and also sell you. Trust is also essential to profitable relationships. This manifesto gives you a ton of great tips on building trust into your key relationships and interactions!

13. The Luck Manifesto

If you ask many famous people or influential leaders how they made their way to the top, more than a few say 'luck'. If you think luck is something you can't control, you're wrong. Whether you call it serendipity, chance, blessings or good fortune, luck plays its part in opening doors and creating chance encounters. This manifesto gives you tips on being more lucky and attracting more good things into your life!

14. The Contra Deal Manifesto

A contra deal is a 'you help me – I help you' arrangement. It's the purest of ways to trade something you've got for something you need. Whether it's influence, resources, introductions, time or advice, your imagination and ability to trade up is one of the most effective ways to accelerate your reputation and leverage your network. And this manifesto shows you how!

15. The Contact Strategy Manifesto

When it comes to your network, how do you decide who is useful and who isn't? There are various ways to classify and calibrate your network. You have strong ties and weak ties, and not knowing which to keep and which to ditch can seriously hold you back. This manifesto will give you a way to evaluate who's good to keep and who needs to go!

16. The Career Sponsor Manifesto

Sponsors are your ultimate career advocates. The right sponsor can almost walk you into the boardroom. They are certainly capable of giving you that extra springboard leap that you need to propel your career forward. This manifesto shows you how to exploit their reputation and connections for promotions, pay rises, book deals and a range of other personal goals!

17. The Personal Board of Advisors Manifesto

Your own carefully crafted Personal Board of Advisors (PBA) is a must for maximum leverage of your networking and reputational assets. In today's complex and uncertain world, no one mentor or advisor is enough. You need input from a range of experts to ensure you get the right experience, wisdom, insight, ideas, perspective and resources. This manifesto fleshes out the strategies in the book to help you recruit your own PBA for maximum career advancement!

18. The Great Questions Manifesto

It's well known that high-quality impactful and insightful questions can open doors to greatness. But what makes a great question? What are the best ones to ask? This manifesto is a really useful guide to shaping and asking higher-quality questions that will bring you respect, reputation and opportunities!

18. The Goal-Setting Manifesto

Everyone has some kind of ambition, but writing down your goals and revisiting them frequently is the only way to keep your goals in sight. It's all about habit and good practice – read this one if you feel this is something you struggle with. You'll get some great insight into the latest thinking on setting goals, as well as why some goals are achieved and some aren't!

19. The Meetings Manifesto

Meetings are a feature of modern corporate and professional life. Everyone is an opportunity to make or break your reputation. Sitting quietly in a meeting will do little to enhance your good name. That's why this manifesto is written especially to help you 'boss' these everyday gatherings for maximum impact!

20. The Telephone Manifesto

The phone remains a formidable relationship and reputation building weapon. In the mobile age, almost everyone is at the end of a phone. Yet many people struggle to speak with impact over the phone. This manifesto will help you improve your telephone manner, leave better voicemail messages and get much more from your phone conversations!

21. The Accountability Manifesto

It's inevitable that you'll develop a few bad habits and make a few wrong decisions in your career. Yet without the perspective and accountability of others, we can get too close and blindsided by all we do. Allowing others to hold you accountable means you'll stay on track, improve your productivity and achieve your goals with greater success. This manifesto gives you those accountability secrets!

22. The Boss Manifesto

Do you know how to make your boss look good? Everyone likes someone that makes him or her look and feel good, why should your boss be any different? It's not a case of being the office suck-up – there are subtle ways to enhance your reputation and 'promotability' by making your boss see how great it is that you are in his or her team. What better way to build your reputation than to have the top dog praise you to others!

23. The Feedback Manifesto

You learn through your mistakes, but part of making those mistakes is also receiving feedback. If you take criticism well, and even solicit it from others, then great. If you don't seek it out and act on it, then you'll struggle to push on, overcome weaknesses and achieve high performance. This manifesto shows you how to put right your wrongs and let people know that they were right to tell you!

24. The Delegation Manifesto

Choosing who is the right person for the job and the right job for the right person is an important aspect of leadership and career advancement. This manifesto gives you powerful delegation tips to help you empower others, lower your workload and build your reputation!

25. The Working Smart Manifesto

It's so easy to waste two hours in the morning sorting your email or post. We all run the risk of getting distracted every time the phone rings. Good systems and processes can prevent this from damaging your productivity. It's simply working smarter, and this manifesto gives you lots of top tips to achieve it. When you get more done, you'll naturally enhance your reputation and make more time to raise your profile!

26. The Habits Manifesto

Good habits are vital in achieving your reputational goals. You can harness your habits for advancement and productivity, or let your habits control you. This manifesto will show you exactly what habits are, how they work and how to use them to accelerate your career and leadership goals!

ABOUT THE AUTHOR

Rob Brown speaks and writes globally on building connections and reputation for greater influence and career opportunities. One of the world's most recommended networking experts according to LinkedIn, Rob interviews other experts all over the world on his Networking Giants Radio Show. A featured TEDx speaker, Rob is founder of the Networking Coaching Academy, a powerful business networking and reputation building training platform.

Rob devised the Networking Success Test™ to help you assess how good you are at networking and compare yourself to the world's best. It's free and you'll get our results instantly. You'll also receive recommendations to improve your networking game. http://networkingcoachingacademy .com/success-test-start

He trains and coaches clients on building collaborative, connected workforces, business networking, partnerships, communicating, relationships, influence, trust, likeability, personal branding and personal reputation building. He lives in Nottingham, UK, the home of Robin Hood, with his wife Amanda and two daughters Georgia and Madison. He has a black belt in kickboxing, loves chocolate and fitness bootcamps, enjoys chess and backgammon, and plays four musical instruments moderately well.

Rob is open to connecting on LinkedIn (therobbrown) so reach out to him and tell him what you think of the book!

rob@rob-brown.com

www.therobbrown.com

ACKNOWLEDGEMENTS

I t's generally easy to do the small stuff, but big projects like this need a team. This means there are always people to thank when you finally get over the line.

I've thanked, blessed, acknowledged and shouted out plenty of people personally for their help and encouragement over the years. Specifically, my best friend and wife Amanda gets huge credit for keeping my life and business going while I did the writing.

My mum will be proud. She always encouraged my writing, so thanks Mum. My pastors Kate, Ali and John deserve credit for investing in me over the years. Dawn and Stu have been hugely generous and supportive from the outset.

I'm blessed to be in two mastermind groups, so big thanks to the guys in Catalyst and Gauntlet for their support and ideas. I appreciate the intro from Warren Cass to Wiley and Capstone, who have been great to work with.

My two daughters Georgia and Madison deserve thanks for their coaching and appreciation which has kept me going.

Finally, I'd like to dedicate this book to my younger brother, Richard, who is no longer with us but inspired many with his positivity, passion and energy. Miss you bro.

INDEX